Writing Inspiration
for Entrepreneurs

55 and 1 content
ideas to turn your
WORDS into SALES

DEBORA LUZI

Founder of
The Writing Academy For Entrepreneurs

Cover image: Lucia G. Garcia
Author image: Beata Nykiel

Published by Goldcrest Books International Ltd
www.goldcrestbooks.com
publish@goldcrestbooks.com

ISBN: 978-1-911505-96-9
eISBN: 978-1-911505-97-6

This book is dedicated to my father, Adriano, who passed away while I was writing this book and whose belief that I am as strong as a mountain will always live in me.

Writing Inspiration for Entrepreneurs is an inspiring, intuitive and talented journey of exploration and discovery to connect with who you truly are and to learn how to embrace your purpose, awaken your true creativity and translate all this into beautifully authentic and impactful written words.

As a business and sales coach, I understand the art and importance of connection in the client journey and this book is a heaven-sent gift for women who want to write powerful and authentic copy and use words that move their audience and create copy that improves their sales success. Debora has created an incredibly unique and soulful space to help you discover the art of excellent writing for business, not to mention inviting you to create a deep and empowering connection between you and your work.

Teresa Brooks
Business & Sales Coach for Women, Founder of COACH Magazine & Podcast

Debora's book is not only fun to read, but a real confidence boost regardless of how successful you already are. She's a true maestro in her ability to tell stories in a way that hits your heart strings and makes you long for more.

The content prompts sprinkled throughout the book are clear, concise and exactly what anyone needs to learn how to express their real voice online. Hesitate no more – there's no way you'll regret reading it and getting to know this powerhouse of a woman better.

Desislava Dobreva
Branding Queen/Recurring Revenue Expert

From the very first sentence in Writing Inspiration for Entrepreneurs *you are taken on a journey of self-discovery and liberation.*

Debora, simply but profoundly, guides you through her process to help you connect with your soul and allow it to speak through your written words. Helping you to express your life story, expertise, and personality to engage with your following on a deeper and more impactful level whilst releasing those fears of being seen.

This Book is where soul meets strategy.

As someone who has been writing content for my business for years, I found myself a little bored and uninspired in my day-to-day writing practise.

This book changed that.

The energy and overall feeling of this book is something I have never experienced from any content creation, marketing book or course.

As I read through each chapter I was almost in tears as more and more inspiration for posts, blogs and the like came rushing through me.

It felt as if I had unlocked a part of me that was hidden away due to conforming to how I felt I should express myself in my business.

I could not put it down, I will re-read and go on this journey again and again.

If you are just starting out in business and looking for inspiration to start connecting with your audience or you are a seasoned entrepreneur looking to express yourself more deeply and impactfully THIS BOOK IS FOR YOU!

Thank you, Debora, for helping me unlock the writer I always knew I was.

Tina Nicola
Founder of Oh My Woo

Debora Luzi shows entrepreneurs how to take the words in their head and turn them into content that will inspire audiences and elicit engagement online.

The prompts in this book will help you discover your writing voice and style your words in a unique and powerful way. Read this book, follow the prompts and take your content to expert status in record time. Say 'Bye! Bye!' to copycat storytelling and start producing content that grabs the attention of buyers (not just fans and followers).

Ungenita Prevost
Founder of FEMME 500 Global International Network & Feminine Leadership Club

CONTENTS

THE BEGINNING OF EVERYTHING

"Debora, 4.5 my dear. I had to ask for help from my husband and children to decipher your essay. I simply could not understand your handwriting".

I've loved writing since I was a child. Writing was a way of escaping a reality which I did not really like and a way of creating imaginary worlds where I would crown myself as the happy and strong heroine.

Words always flew easily through me and for this reason my Italian literature teacher could not understand my handwriting. Words and ideas were coming to me as fast as a tornado, so in case I would forget them, I had to write them down as fast as I could, often with indecipherable handwriting.

I remember writing a book about my extensive backpacking travelling in more than 20 countries at the age of 22. I had this dream of becoming an author and sharing my inspiring story with the world. Unfortunately, my handwritten book was stolen from my bag from a locker while I was working at a tile shop.

I was devastated. I did not care about the beautiful bag, the wallet, the money inside the wallet, my half-empty make-up case. All I cared for was my lost handwritten book.

I tried to write that book again years later, but the half-written manuscript still sits on my library shelf, full of dust and memories which I struggled to remember to the smallest details.

I always felt that burning desire inside, of writing my book.

And so here I am writing my second book following an intuitive hit I received today while travelling on a train out of London.

I cannot recall the number of diaries I have written since I was 8 years old. The white papers and the pen truly became my best friends.

I stopped writing for a while when I emigrated to London to work as an au-pair and learn the English language. My lack of fluency in this new language was limiting my ability to fully express myself and at the same time was making me forget some of the words and expressions in my native language. I felt so frustrated for a long time, unable to decide what language I was going to write in. I felt as if I no longer belonged to a language and a country.

Years later after taking many courses and passing many exams in the English language, I was given an opportunity to write again while working as an events and marketing manager. But again, my writing was not fitting the "usual" standards. My former boss thought it was too informal and not "good enough".

I started to truly believe that "my writing voice" had no place in this world and that it was not meant to be expressed and freed.

After much disappointment and lack of belief in my role of writer, I was forced to write again many years later after leaving my corporate job and venturing into the entrepreneurial world.

I say I was forced but what I mean is that I had to force myself to write and put myself out there.

When I started my business, I had no money to pay a copy writer or even someone that would proofread my writing. I had to roll up my sleeves and start writing.

At first, I felt very shy to show up on social media with my content, tell the world about what I was passionate about or simply say who I was. I had so many fears of being judged and criticised. I would often just read other people's comments and refrain from commenting and giving my opinion for fear of making mistakes, saying the wrong things and being booed. I still recall the many times I started to comment on someone else's content when I was disagreeing with it and pressing the left-pointing arrow on the keyboard until every word I had written would just disappear.

I remember toning down my whole world, my whole way of expressing myself, my sense of humour, my loving sarcasm, and my extravagant nature. My content looked like a sad clown, who had forced himself to wear the most boring, lifeless mask to fit in, hide and not be noticed too much.

It took me a while to finally find and own my voice and take my place in the entrepreneurial world. When I eventually did and ditched all the fears, I started to receive much praise. People were telling me they would never skip past my content as it was very inspiring, motivating and entertaining.

As you would expect the good comments and praise came accompanied by negative and critical comments too, mainly referring to the wrong use of grammar or spelling mistakes.

I went through a big internal battle, doubting myself and reminding myself that I was simply a 4.5 girl in the end.

What was I trying to achieve? What was I trying to prove?

I recall that day, after receiving other comments both positive and negative, being totally devoured by frustration and excitement at the same time. I froze for a moment, unsure and uncertain about my next step.

While trying to figure it out, grabbing onto any random ideas my mind would focus on, I decided to join a writing school or a writing academy so as to become a better writer and please "my audience" even more. I now had an audience so I had to make sure to deliver the best possible content to them. I had set some high standards for myself and I was determined to reach them.

While searching for a writing school online, I remember hearing a soft but strong whisper coming from above my head which said to me, "Debora, open a writing academy, you are already a good and creative writer, do it now!"

"What?" I remember saying to myself, totally puzzled at the idea.

"Me, open a writing academy?" I was shocked, scared, and a bit fearful but at the same time, I felt a strong wave of excitement running through me and I started to fall in love with this beautiful and crazy idea.

Above all, I had always listened to my intuition so I could not fail to do it now.

One of my life mottos to that day had always been, "When the whisper speaks, follow." I had no choice but to follow it.

Within minutes I found myself brainstorming a few names for the writing academy. I did not want a name which was too fancy, or which would not make my audience understand what the community was about. I wanted a simple, straightforward, "it does what it says on the tin" name.

After the very straightforward name was born, I went to create a banner on Canva and opened a special group for it.

I jotted down on paper some marketing content, published it on a few online platforms and, to my astonishment, I had already 3 paying members after only 2 hours of putting the content out there.

I could never doubt the whispers. They always know exactly what is best for me and what is my next step to take. All they do is guide me by dropping little intuitive crumbs to show me the way.

And The Writing Academy for Entrepreneurs was conceived. The only online community for entrepreneurs focused on writing unique, authentic and engaging content that connects, converts and impacts using the power of intuition, heart and a dose of strategies.

The rest is history!

One of the first and main features of the academy was to provide weekly content ideas through a prompt which I delivered twice a week. I still do.

Many entrepreneurs find it challenging to show up, write for their business and most of all to sell themselves and their products and services. So they prefer not to show up at all and consequently don't make enough sales in their business.

Something I realised since becoming an entrepreneur is that writing for your business does not need to be boring and time-consuming.

Writing for your business can be much more fun and easy if you are willing to tap into your own creative genius and let the fears of judgement and criticism leave the show!

I have collected some of my best writing content ideas from The Writing Academy for Entrepreneurs to help you show up powerfully and authentically with your content so that your soul client (more about what a soul client is later) can start falling in love with you, trusting you and ultimately buying from you.

I am sure you will enjoy these prompts as much as I did writing them, and as much as The Writing Academy members love them. Each week, they impatiently wait for another one to be released.

We currently have over 181 writing prompts in the academy, a number which will have gone right up by the time you are reading this book as I write two new ones each week.

I have selected 55 and 1 for you today.

Grab pen and paper, it is time to unleash your writing beast and let your writing genius take the rein. Your audience and readers are waiting for your words and content to help them change and improve their lives.

No more delays. They have been waiting for too long for you to show up and own your writing voice.

Are you ready to write as if nobody is watching?

I am sure you are from the moment you picked up this book.

Debora Luzi
Founder of The Writing Academy for Entrepreneurs

I want to explain to you an expression I often use in this book and in my business.

SOUL CLIENT

What do I mean by soul client?

Soul client is another powerful way of describing your "ideal client". I call it soul client as I believe you are already connected to all of your clients at a higher level. It is as if you are connected to your soul clients by an invisible thread.

Your and your client's soul are already speaking and making connections even before you actually become aware of this in your consciousness.

Your soul client is the client whose path is meant to meet yours, because you are one of the instruments that will help them to achieve their dreams and fulfil their mission.

Your soul client is the perfect client for you, the client with whom working happens with ease and synchronicity.

Your soul client is the client that fires your heart up because you have a bigger desire to help them on their path and you will likewise light their fire up as you will be the catalyst for them, the one showing them and guiding them on their journey, regardless of how long.

MEDITATION

I do not believe in people not being creative or in the so-called "writer's block".

I strongly believe we are all equally creative and imaginative if we allow ourselves to be.

The word "allow" here is key.

Not being able to write is often caused by fears and conditioning that people impose on themselves, addiction to perfection and fear of offending others and not being liked.

Let me go deeper into this concept.

Imagine you get an idea to write a piece of content. You get excited, you grab a pen and paper and you start writing. Words are flowing like a soft gentle wind; the inspiration is at its glory.

You keep writing when, suddenly, you stop and read it back. Doubts start to creep in. You start to doubt your own writing because you project onto it what others might think of it.

"Mmm, I might change that sentence as Mary might be offended"

"I think this concept is not going to be understood in the right way, let's delete it altogether"

"My former boss might read this and disapprove of it"

"I might be shamed for this"

All those thoughts are softly killing the beautiful writing momentum you have created. You start doubting yourself. You start to cross out words or press the delete button in half of your content.

What happens is that this beautiful piece of writing, which came straight from your intuition and from your heart, is now turned into a fearful "fit in the box" piece of content.

The real essence of it has gone, its real flavour can no longer be tasted.

Destined to disappear in the world of social media as another boring, lifeless copycat piece of content, which does not serve its original purpose or the people who were ready to read it, it makes its entrance from the back door, unnoticed, unseen, misunderstood.

I was very much the person going back and forth to my content and pressing the delete button all the time. I cannot recall the number of times that I have modified, taken out, added words to my content just to please the masses, allowing the piece to lose its beauty and purpose.

It is my biggest passion to teach you how to write from your intuition and your heart without fear, without modifying anything or very, very little. Remember you are not writing to please everyone; you are writing to please the ones who will resonate with your message and be moved by it.

Do not adapt your content to your audience. The right audience will find you.

It is my deepest desire for you to start writing from your intuition and your heart so that your words and content can stand out more, attract the right audience and inspire people every day.

I have created a beautiful meditation to help you do this, which I am going to share with you.

This meditation will awaken your intuition, help you to profoundly connect to your heart and its desires and write in total flow as a consequence.

◈ Before we start please go and grab a pen and hold it on your right hand

◈ Sit comfortably in a quiet place. Make sure you will not be distracted for at least 10 minutes

◈ Gently close your eyes and take three big breaths

◈ Breathe in and breathe out

◈ As you breathe in and out focus your attention in the now. You are here, sitting down, your body touching the floor or the chair. You can hear noises from outside. You can hear the noise of your own mind

◈ There is no yesterday, not a moment or an hour ago. There is no tomorrow, or later. All there is, is NOW. Right here in this exact moment

◈ Become aware of what is around you and what is in you

◈ Now focus your attention into the middle of your eyes, in the third eye chakra (chakra is a centre of energy in our body, which means 'wheels' in Sanskrit). Hold a pen in your right hand and put it into this point and start spinning your hand clockwise, making small circles

◈ As you spin, imagine a strong purple light entering this area, and as you spin imagine hearing your intuition speaking to you. Your intuition is the voice of your higher self, which knows exactly what is best for you in your life. The voice that is not subject to limitations or conditionings, the voice of your soul

◈ Carefully listen to those voices or whispers. As your hand spins, you hear the voices, the whispers get louder and clearer

◈ What are they telling you? Are they giving you ideas, thoughts, actions to take?

◈ Let them flow into you with no judgement

◈ As you keep spinning your hand in circles, you hear more and more whispers. You are ready to listen

◈ Now repeat out loud or in your mind, "Thank you, I am ready to listen, I am ready to allow my intuition to speak to me and guide me, and so it is, and so it is, and so it is."

◈ Now gently move your hand to your heart area. Start spinning your hand clockwise and make small circles. As you spin your hand imagine connecting to your heart. Hear its beat, "tu tum. Tu tum," imagine you and your heart becoming one

◇ With each spin hear your heart speaking to you. Be open to listening to it. What does your heart want to tell you? What are your heart's desires? What are the feelings and emotions that your heart feels right now? What are the feelings and emotions, the stories that your heart secretly hides?

◇ Be ready to listen

◇ Remain silent for a few minutes and simply listen and feel

◇ Connect to every single emotion stored in your heart, even the ones you might feel ashamed of. The secret ones, the ones you are trying to forget and hide. There cannot be shame in your heart as every emotion you felt or are still feeling is part of your journey and made you who you are today. Own your journey, your story and all the emotions and memories attached to it. Know deep in your heart that gold can be found in all the scars you carry

◇ Now repeat out loud or in your mind, "I am ready to listen to you, I am ready to feel, and I am ready to be, and so it is and so it is and so it is."

◇ Feel the warmth of your heart in your hand and feel this beautiful connection between you and your heart

◇ Now put your left hand into your third eye and your right hand to your heart and slowly bring them together into your mouth (the area of your throat chakras, where your real voice comes from, where your truth is spoken)

◈ Imagine the whispers from your third eye and the desires and the feelings from your heart all joining together into the mouth or throat chakra area, ready to be freed and expressed.

◈ Open your mouth wide and make a strong and firm "ahhhh" sound, letting all these words come out of you, ready to be expressed and ready to be written onto paper

◈ Get them all out, sound "ahhhhhh" a few times until all the words have imaginably come out

◈ Take three deep breaths, put your feet firm on the ground to ground yourself and gently open your eyes

You are ready to write your truth now.

You are ready to write with your true voice, no more excuses.

I have recorded this meditation for you so that you can listen to it anytime you need some writing inspiration.

You can download it from this link:
www.deboraluzi.com/meditation

THE ART OF BECOMING YOUR OWN CONTENT WRITER

"Why become my own content writer when there are so many people out there ready to write for me and my business?" you may ask.

The response is very simple.

Because no one can write as you do, no one can know you as much as you do, and no one can relive your stories as passionately and lively as yourself.

I am not rejecting the work of content writers; I simply want to encourage entrepreneurs to show up more with their very own content in order to connect to their audience at a much deeper level.

Your audience needs to hear the real you, your thoughts and HEAR YOU FULLY in order to deeply connect to you, trust you and ultimately buy from you.

You could have a content writer writing pieces for you, but not everything. Make sure you show up with some of your own content every week.

I am so glad you bought this book as it will help you create those beautiful pieces of content you are dreaming of writing.

Writing for your business is not about hiding behind words already written on your website, or the results you are delivering.

Writing for your business is about taking your audience on a beautiful journey of self-discovery by using different types of content which engages, motivates and entertains.

Writing for your business is more about telling your audience WHO you are rather than what you do and what you offer.

I love to personally inspire and entertain my audience through my content and tell them all about WHO I truly am.

What about you?

Stop for a moment and ask yourself this question; "What purpose do I want to give to my writing?"

What do I want to gift others through my writing?

What do I want them to receive and feel?

Having an intention is key.

Every time I write a piece of content, I ask myself "Why am I putting this piece of content out there?"

"What is the specific result I want to achieve?"

Do I want to motivate people to take action? Do I want to increase my authority in my field, increase my following, offer my products and services or show pieces of me that my audience crave to know about?

Setting an intention and adding a pinch of strategic targeting to your content are paramount if you want to set the right energy and "hit" the target.

Where the intention is set, energy flows.

You now may ask, "How on earth do you come up with so many different ideas for content every day?"

The answer is pretty easy.

I want you to understand that anything can become a piece of content, and anything can give you a reason to start writing.

This is exactly how I never run out of content ideas. I turn everything that happens to me daily into a piece of content.

Stories, conversations with my children, conversations with strangers at the supermarket, phrases from billboards, articles I read, thoughts that run through my mind (and no excuses here as human beings go through 6,000 thoughts a day[1], so you would have 6,000 potential writing ideas at your fingertips daily, how crazy is that).

I once wrote an article about a phrase I read during my son's secondary school visit.

"Attitude determines altitude". I developed the story, gave my own opinion and shared my experience with it.

Another time I was travelling on a bus when I saw a billboard advertising a particular university. The phrase really caught my eyes. It said something like, "Are you choosing that university because your parents want you to?"

---

1. https://www.dailymail.co.uk/sciencetech/article-8531913/Average-person-6-000-thoughts-day-according-study-isolated-thought-worm.html

I took a picture of the bus and later on I wrote a beautiful piece of content discussing how many people in life do what others want them to do or expect them to do. I gave my own personal input and experience. The content was a great success.

Other times I simply ask a question or expand on conversations I have had with my husband or close friends.

You may think that you are in business here and that type of content will NOT interest your audience. Think again.

Remember that your audience will want to hear you, feel you, know what you think of and believe in to connect with you at a deeper level and start trusting you.

Why do you think reality TV shows are so popular? Because people want to feel closer to others, they want to relate to them, and feel as if they belong to something they choose to follow.

Your audience will want to know that you are REAL, that you are like them to a certain extent, with your ups and downs and your vulnerability.

I cannot recall the amount of times I've heard people saying, "I bought from you, Debora, because you are real because I feel connected to you."

While you may struggle every day to filter words and content which you think will attract the right audience, start digging within, share those thoughts, share your knowledge and expertise and SHOW UP as powerfully as you truly are.

When you do that, writing will no longer feel like a chore but like one of the most beautiful ways to express yourself and to help others.

I often hear people saying that writing content for their business feels boring and daunting. The reason is that people are trying to filter too much, to correct too much to hide too much.

When we write with the purest intention to motivate and inspire others through our words, writing will feel empowering and easy.

When you are truly connected to your purpose, you love what you are doing and you have a massive desire to help others, there are NO WORDS that can stop you from doing that. The only person that can stop you is yourself.

Imagine going to visit a friend who is not feeling very well and is going through a difficult time. I am sure you would not be short of words to help her or him, motivate her or offer a possible solution. So why when you go and write a piece of content, where you can do exactly the same, are you suddenly short of words and do not know what to say?

The main reason is that you step out of your heart, you lose the main focus and you focus on the fears of judgment instead. You have simply jumped from your heart to your controlling mind.

People need to hear your message. They will not mind if it is not perfect or if there is a small mistake.

People who need to hear your message will not be demotivated because the message is not perfect and say, "Oh she has made a mistake, I do not feel motivated now! I am out of here."

They will read your message, feel your message and desire and respond positively to it.

Your audience will FEEL your energy and intention behind your words, so it is important that you write from that intention in your heart.

Your words will be heard, will heal, will be shared when they come from that space.

I invite you to start writing as if nobody is watching, in the same way you will speak to your friends or children, in the same way you passionately write your journal, because the energy you do this with is WHAT will make a difference.

We have a saying in Italy which goes: *"Parla come mangia"* which means "speak as you eat". And I would like to add "Speak and WRITE as you eat. If you are a messy eater, do not pretend to eat like royals. If you are a fast, aggressive eater, do not pretend to eat while chanting OMssssss."

Be 100% who you are.

One of the best compliments I received in business was this one from a woman who said to me after meeting me in person and following me for some time: "You are exactly the same, online and off. Funny, sarcastic and very charming."

Has it ever happened to you meeting someone in person and having a great conversation with them, only to doubt later on when you check their website, whether or not you are reading about the same person?

I am sure it did happen to you as it has happened to me many times.

Make sure you are not two different versions of yourself in two different places.

And if your mind is whispering something to you such as "But I cannot possibly show up the same way in all the places, some places require me to be more formal, or "professional" or......"

Remember what I mentioned in the previous chapter: "Do not adapt your content to your audience. The right audience will find you."

When you have this clear in your mind, you will realise that you can be who you are and "write as you eat" everywhere you go.

THE 5 WRITING PERSONALITIES TO WRITE YOUR CONTENT WITH

Now that we have established how easy it can be to become your own content writer and how to give an intention to your writing, let's go deep into this writing journey which requires you to embody 5 different writing personalities.

We are not going to invent or create anything new. I truly believe all these different writing personalities are already in you. What we are going to do is awaken them in you and bring them to the light.

Some of them will come more naturally to you than others. Some might require a bit of more courage and boldness from your side. Some you might be frightened to discover.

I want you to allow yourself the freedom to experience them all, without fear or judgement, knowing that you have been them many times before, without even realising.

Some of them will come more naturally than others because they will feel more comfortable, hence others will feel scary because you will need to go deep within and drop into your heart.

I strongly encourage you to write content from the ones which feel more daunting and apprehensive at first. You want to eat the ugly frog first and get it out of the way. And when you do, know in your heart that you have just overcome one of your fears.

I believe that when we overcome our own fears, we simply transmute their energy into power which we can use to our own advantage.

We are now going to explore those writing personalities. Be aware that one could not exist without the other and that all of them are fundamental to helping you write strong content that will attract the right people, engage them and help you sell your products and services to them with ease.

Are you ready? Fasten your seat belt, grab a pen and paper and let's start this journey.

DISCOVERER

One of the most important principles of writing for your business is knowing exactly WHO YOU ARE because if you do not, how can your audience know who you are hence connecting and resonating with you?

Knowing who you are means bringing all that you are into your writing; your ideas, your style, your flavours, your uniqueness and your passions.

Knowing who you are will help you find your very own UNIQUE writing voice. You do not want to write like Mary's or John's voice just because they are successful, and they have given you their formulas. You want to write and sound like you so that your audience can recognise you even if you do not sign your content or add a picture of yourself to it.

You want to stand out with your own writing voice.

I get people telling me all the time that they recognise my content from miles away even if I do not mark it or sign it.

Why? Because every time I write I make sure I write in my own unique writing style, which all of us have if we allow it to emerge from within.

My writing voice is rather informal, conversational, funny and sarcastic at times. I write with excitement, with passion and I love to tell stories using suspense, curiosity and direct speech.

When I started my business, I did not own my writing voice. I thought it was too informal and sarcastic so I pretended to sound like someone else, and guess what?

That did not work at all. The few clients I attracted did not resonate with my energy at all, hence it was very difficult to work with them. I felt exhausted as I felt I had to put on a show and a mask each time and pretend to be someone I was not.

How can you find your own writing voice?

Start asking yourself these questions:

- ✐ How do I speak when I am around friends?

- ✐ What words, sentences, catchy phrases, metaphors do I like to use?

- ✐ How do I write when I write in my diary or my journal, knowing that no one will read it?

- ✐ What am I passionate about? Music? Art? Colours?

Think of how you can bring those passions of yours into your writing. For instance, if you like cooking, perhaps you can use cooking terms in your content, and engage the sense of taste. You could use this with any business you may have, even if you are an accountant. Maybe you can write about the perfect recipe to complete your tax return on time? By adding, whisking, mixing certain "ingredients" or qualities.

Perhaps you like music and you want to start using content from songs, or insert "singing noises" into your content?

Is this becoming clearer to you?

Remember there are no rules when it comes to finding your writing voice, there is no right or wrong.

Or perhaps you like to use words Like oops, bang! splash! when you speak, so why don't you insert them in your content?

To help you with discovering who you are, I want to give you a special writing prompt.

Write the words: I AM....and start writing all that you are.

Maybe you are the mother and daughter, maybe you are the strong hurricane which does not let anyone influence you. Maybe you are a delicate flower ready to blossom...

Embrace all that you are. Start writing.

It is time you show the world who you are and let them know through your very unique writing voice.

STORYTELLER

You might not be surprised to see this on the list. Humankind has evolved, thrived, grown through stories. Stories connect, unite and divide, stories engage the mind and the heart. Stories are remembered for years to come.

I have been to many events, heard many speakers on stage and if you are to tell me what I remember about those events and talks, I can easily tell you that all I remember is the stories told.

I always patiently wait for the speaker to tell their stories. I am not interested in their products, in what they are saying, if I do not know where they have come from, what brought them to do what they do and why they are doing it.

So many of my clients work or have worked with me because of my story which they have read and resonated with. My story often was the final decision that made them buy from me.

Your business coach and mentor has probably already told you to share your story in one way or another.

Stories are shared, but often not in the right way or not enough times to build that deeper connection needed for your audience to buy from you.

Your story shared just on your website is not enough. It is important that you share your story very often with your audience, at least weekly.

Sharing your story is not about a cold chronicle of the facts which happened or a cold narrative of some crucial moments you might have had.

Sharing your story is about bringing to life the feelings, the emotions you felt, describing them in such a vivid way that your audience can almost FEEL them with you.

Another important aspect of sharing your story is sharing a piece of your story and not your entire storyline, from the moment you were born to the moment of where you are now. Writing stories for social media or for an article is not like writing a book. Your story needs to be specific, concise, it needs to have a trail and not run wild everywhere. You do not want to confuse your audience; you want them to follow the story and engage with it.

I give some very useful exercises in my Writing Academy for Entrepreneurs to identify those stories from your life timeline, the ones that have marked the biggest transformations in your life related to what you do right now in your business.

Let me invite you to recall a piece of your story where you had one of the biggest wakeup calls in life. A story that made you who you are today, a story that shaped and formed you.

The secret here is to engage your audience and make them stop by, so in order to do that start the story with a very compelling heading, one that inspires curiosity and does not give too much away at the same time....

'Once upon a time' stories are not accepted here, they are for books and not for social media.

You want to make sure you keep your audience glued to your story. The first way is by attracting them with a very curious headline, the second way is to not give away the main plot in the second paragraph. If you do, they will be out of the story in a flash as now they know what happens.

So, use the second paragraph to set the scene, to introduce the characters briefly, (remember you are writing for social media and not for a book), then slowly unfold the story and the main crucial moment, the moment of big change, the moment you kept your audience waiting for.

Always make sure to share any stories from the victorious side and not the victim side. You want to share stories to motivate and inspire others, to give a lesson and not to make people feel sorry for you.

It is important that you deliver a specific message at the end. I call this the " ribbon' of the story.

Ask yourself this question: " What message, lessons do I want to deliver to my audience with this story?"

And once you are clear on that message, make sure you wrap your beautiful story in it.

So, let's write a story today. Start writing choosing one of these headings:

- I never thought that it could happen to me
- That was the moment that everything changed for me

🖉 I stood there thinking..." How did I get myself into this mess?"

🖉 Feel free to make up your very own one.

TEACHER

I don't know about you, but one of my big dreams as a child was to become a teacher and share all my knowledge with others. There is a certain fascination around being a teacher and listening to a teacher when you are hungry for more knowledge.

Becoming the teacher and embodying this type of personality is very important when you write for your business.

Your readers will want to see you as an expert, and they will more likely follow you and read your content if they know they are learning something from you.

Writing as a teacher is your opportunity to show your audience that you know what you are talking about, that you are the expert in your field and it is your opportunity to give advice, share tips and secrets that can change your reader's life.

I encourage you to write as a teacher very often. You could, for instance, share the number one secret that has helped you or your clients to go from A to B, or the 5 steps to easily attract more clients or the 3 secrets to a lasting relationship.

No wonder many online publications ask their contributors to write articles with these types of content. Humans are naturally curious and would do anything to know what happens next. When you entitle a piece of writing with "the

3 secrets to......" your reader will feel curious and will have an urge to want to know what these secrets are.

Do you know that many people who watch a video where 3 or 5 secrets are shared, fast forward the video to know the 3 or 5 secrets and then they are out in a flash as soon as they know them?

Also, this type of content is educative, engaging and easy to read.

You can use different headlines. For instance, "the number one step that helped my client to go from 0 attendees at his/her event to a sold-out event" or "The number one mistake I made in my business you do not want to make"

Now is your turn.

I want you to stop for a moment and start gathering all of your knowledge and expertise. What tips, advice, piece of information can you share with your audience today?

Perhaps the 3 secrets to happiness? Or how to sleep better in 3 easy steps or...?

When you write a teaching piece of content make sure you go deep into the details, do not simply share three words, like eat, sleep and meditate. Go deep into the process and make sure to give plenty of value.

Here are some ideas for you:

✐ How you can go from A to B by applying these steps

✐ The 5 steps to

✐ The 3 secrets to

🖉 How to overcome X in 4 easy, affordable, low cost, effective etc ways

Your readers will love to learn from you and they will surely come back for more.

LEADER

I want you to think about any leader in history you strongly admire.

Maybe it's Mother Teresa, or Martin Luther King or Nelson Mandela or Greta Thunberg or Barack Obama.

Let me ask you, why do you admire them or follow them?

Have a think. I am sure one of the reasons is because they strongly stand for something, they believe in a particular cause and are ready to stick by their convictions, no matter what.

Leaders are by nature very mentally strong people who are not easily influenced or persuaded.

Your audience must see that in you too. People do not like "fluffy" leaders, people who are all over the place and that hold no morals or beliefs of their own.

Your audience likes to see that you strongly stand for something and that your opinion is not easily influenced or manipulated.

As a business owner and entrepreneur it is important to take the position of a leader. Your audience needs to see and become aware of your views and your opinions.

So today, I will ask you to....STAND UP!

Yes, if you are sitting down, please stand up with your chest open and your head high and start to give a voice to the causes that your heart feels passionate about.

Whatever sets your heart on fire, talk about it, stand by it and believe in it.

Whatever that is, maybe you stand for equality and inclusion, or animal welfare or you are against child trafficking. Perhaps you have your own opinion about something that is happening right now in the world or in your industry. Do not change your opinions or ideas to fit that of your audience. Speak up, be you and then your audience will find you.

I want to ask you this question. What do you strongly believe in? What causes do you support? What drives you insane in the world or in your industry?

Take a few minutes to find the answers to these questions and then go and talk about it, write content about it, articles or blogs.

I wanted to share with you my personal journey of writing as a leader.

When I started to write in the online world, I felt very shy and insecure. I felt my voice and my opinions had no space in the online world as there was so much going on already. I remember reading content that would make my blood boil but never finding the courage to reply or give my perspective as I was afraid to be attacked, judged and criticised.

It took me a while to find my voice and claim my space in the online, writing world.

Humans' number one fear is that of not being liked or accepted, to be excluded, judged and to not belong. So expressing your true opinion about something can be very daunting as you will certainly have people who do not agree with you, who will attack you and perhaps call you names.

My first encounter with expressing my opinion about something was around 4 years ago. I remember delivering an online challenge, called the "Daring Challenge". The challenge consisted in doing something daring every day for 5 days. One of the tasks on day 4 was to write a piece of content about something you strongly disagree with. I had this opinion about something ready to be expressed, but I always felt fearful to express it because of the reaction it would cause.

That day I found all my courage and wrote a piece of content of my disagreement with women wanting their husbands to retire before their time and be the only one to work and bring the money home.

Pressing the send button was very hard that day. I gathered all my courage, closed my eyes and put the content out there.

I then left for a walk.

When I got back to the content there were a few negative comments, some people jumped on the content saying that they did not agree, and of course many people were also sharing the same view as mine.

This is normal. There is no shame in your beliefs and your ideas even if they go against what most people think.

This might seem like a small thing to you, but at the beginning of my journey I was very scared to say anything that people would disagree with, so this seemed very big to me.

I want you to understand that we are in a world with 8 billion other people. Each and every single one of us has a different thinking, often based on our experience and beliefs, the way we were raised and the experiences we have lived. Consequently, it is impossible to think that 8 billion people can think exactly the same as you and have the same opinions about something. That is why the world is full of different groups, communities, parties, religions and theories to confirm this diversity of thoughts, opinions of humankind.

You cannot expect to please the masses with your content in order to be liked. Someone, somewhere will always disagree with you, not like you or dislike what you are saying. Hence it is so much better to speak your truth and stand tall and strong next to what you believe in rather than trying to please the masses and hide your truth.

Today I want to invite you to create a piece of content where you strongly express your opinion about something or your view on a particular cause.

Go back to the questions I have asked you above and start writing, then put it out there, and before you do make sure you own that piece of writing and strongly believe in it.

I want to be clear on something here. Writing like a leader is not about becoming a keyboard warrior and having endless wars on social media, or any other platforms, with people because they do not think like you do. It is simply about standing in your truth and being OK with the fact that not everyone will agree with you.

SALESPERSON

I had a lot of fun with developing this last writing personality. I am being a bit sarcastic here as I used to absolutely hate it, and I am sure you did too at some stage in your business, and you might still do.

Many entrepreneurs enter the entrepreneurial world hating selling and feeling totally uncomfortable with it. The point is that if you do not sell or feel ashamed by it you are not helping anyone, including yourself. If I ask you why you started your own business, I am sure most of you will say that the reason is because you want to help others overcome a particular problem which you might have faced before.

The truth is, if you do not go out there and tell people that you are open for business by proposing to them, telling them what you are actually selling, inviting them to buy, they will think you simply show up because you have nothing to do all day and your business is just a hobby.

I cannot recall the number of times that my clients told me they are lost because they tried everything - showing up every single day, doing endless live videos, following all the gurus and having the perfect website.

When I go and check their profiles and content, all I see is endless "content", without a single sale. Most people think that simply showing up, having a website link and a booking link is enough to get clients. No, no, no! Absolutely not!

It is a must that you sell to your audience, that you write sales content, that you sell through your content all the time.

If that feels uncomfortable, it is time you drop from your head to your heart again.

When selling feels uncomfortable you are in your head. You fear being considered salesy, pushy, you fear being judged. You make it all about yourself and your fears while you forget that you are in business not for yourself or your ego but to help others and make an impact in the world one person at the time.

It is my most sincere wish to make you understand that selling is the only way to help others.

If you are feeling still uncomfortable, I want you to know that I hear you completely. I remember avoiding the word "sales" all the time. I recall going into sales conversations and talking about everything but the sales. I would ask how the dog, or the cat were doing, or give compliments every 5 minutes, or talk about the weather. I simply could not invite people to buy from me.

I often even felt sick at the thought of it. I thought I would not stand a chance to make sales in my business until I dropped to my heart, connected to it and made it about my audience and not me.

I now sell with ease and I love it. Selling has become so natural to me that sometimes I sell without even realising it. I know my products and services can change lives, enrich lives so I get so passionate about telling the world about it.

I want you to know that if you fear people judging you for selling, these are not your clients in the first place, full stop.

There is something important I want to bring to your attention. If you feel uncomfortable with being sold to, you will feel uncomfortable to sell to others and you will find it challenging.

Being sold to and selling comes from the same energy. People who are selling are simply following their passion and mission. Yes, I agree, there are many people out there who sell without integrity, but they do not have to influence you or make you hate selling altogether. That is simply their way, not yours.

Selling with love and passion can only be received with love by the people who are ready to receive it.

The more you relax about the fact that other people will be selling to you, the easier it will become for you to sell. If you receive someone else's sale with doubts and fears, your sales will be perceived with doubts and fears.

Saying that, I want to invite you to sell with your content very often. When I am in launch mode, I sell every day using different types of content. I create sales content out of stories, testimonials, quotes, you name it. You need to become creative and a bit strategic when it comes to writing sales content.

I always try to write a variety of sales content, some more direct, some less direct.

When you write sales content make sure you add these fundamental pieces in it:

✎ be clear on who the target audience is for that particular product/service

✎ be clear on the benefits of the products by being super specific. Saying that this product will help people feel better or feel more empowered is not enough. You need to ask yourself this question "What does it mean that client X will feel empowered?" "How would they know they are empowered, how would their life change once they are empowered?"

🖉 be clear on what the actual offer is

🖉 be clear on the instructions on how to buy that particular offer

🖉 make sure you add urgency and scarcity. This means to add an expiration date to the offer or a limited number of people. Yes, this is very mainstream, but it works.

Something I am very passionate about teaching in my academy is targeting the consequences of the problem and not the problem itself. Let me give you a few examples. Let's say you help people get more clients, you will not address the issue of not having clients in your sales content but you will address the *consequences* of not having clients.

For instance, the consequences could be that your soul client constantly argues with their spouse because they are not bringing enough money home, so they feel pushed to go back to a corporate job.

Or let's say the problem is being single and finding it really challenging to find 'the one'. You will not address the "being single" but you will address the consequences of being single which could be: refusing your friend's weekend gathering because everyone will have a partner and you are dead tired of showing up alone.

These are just examples to give you an idea.

Maybe start to write down some of these consequences. They will massively help you to make your message much more specific and hit home for many of the readers.

Often your soul client will not even realise they have "the problem" you solve, but they will recognise themselves in the "consequence scenario" you are describing.

I am feeling very optimistic knowing that you are probably starting to love selling and you cannot wait to write some sales content.

HOW TO BEST USE THE WRITING PROMPTS

There are many ways in which you can use the 55 and 1 writing prompts in this book.

The prompts are not only writing ideas, many of them offer true value to you, helping you to think outside the box, explore parts of you and your story that will help you connect to your audience.

Many will invite you to unleash your creativity, and others are ideas and suggestions on why it's best to use a certain type of content instead of another.

Others will help you to become crystal clear on your soul client language and on creating a clear message that appeals to them.

I have left some lined spaces after each prompt for you to write.

Once you read the prompt, grab a pen and start writing. Do not overthink, simply let the words flow through you, out of you. Write as if nobody is watching. Write as if you were having a conversation with your best friend about that particular topic, I ask you to write about.

You may want to read them all in one go and then go back to them, or you may want to read one a day and start writing it straight away. You may put the content out there on social media or create a blog from it or an article for a magazine or an online publication.

Remember there are no strict rules when we write from our intuition and our heart.

A fun way you could approach the prompts, is to simply pick a number and then go to the corresponding page in the book and see which prompt corresponds to the number you randomly picked and start writing.

You could also plan your weekly content based on the following prompts.

You can use them over and over again, get inspired by them and write different content and ideas each time.

I often go back to a particular prompt twice and the content is never the same.

I believe we are never the same in two different moments, as we constantly evolve.

At the end of each prompt I have given you a guideline on which writing personality you could write the prompts from. Sometimes you could use a prompt as a story for instance, engaging the storyteller, or other times you could write it as sales content, engaging the writing personality of the salesperson.

I want to encourage you to be creative with them, to play and to not get stuck with too much "should "in your mind. Simply write.

Also do not write them just for yourself. Start to put whatever you write out there. Do not keep it a secret. If you are an introvert and you have never written for your business before, this is the time to start. Remember that you are writing for a bigger purpose and that you need to start somewhere. After that first step you take, the rest will feel much easier, I promise you.

If you are already writing and putting content out there, these prompts can help you create more content and show your audience a different version of yourself. A more real, rawer version of you. The more you show how real you are, the bigger the connection you will build with your audience.

I often see entrepreneurs putting content out there which is too perfect and too polished. Do you know what are the consequences of doing this? A lack of connection and engagement from the reader.

I love to share with my audience the real me, the real "no" moments that I might experience at a particular time, the doubts and the fears that I am experiencing during my journey.

I remember being overwhelmed with doubts in the middle of organising my first ever women's conference. I felt scared, overwhelmed, I doubted if I could truly deliver such a big event.

Instead of hiding those feelings, I wrote several beautiful pieces of content revealing how I was feeling inside, showing my audience that I am human too in the end. When I share those moments of doubts and fear I always make sure to deliver a positive message and any learnings in the end. I never share them to get "pity" or attention but to inspire and motivate others.

Many of the prompts will encourage you to talk about yourself, your story, your journey and not only what you are selling. Your audience needs to hear that first.

If you are running a business and you most likely are the face of your brand, your audience must get familiar with the person behind the brand. And the only way to do that is by getting personal.

I am not suggesting you need to become a total open book and jeopardise your privacy. In the end you are the one always choosing what to share, how to share and how much of it to share.

What I suggest is that you let your audience see, feel and hear the person behind your personal brand.

It is my greatest wish for you to start sharing pieces of you, pieces of your story and journey with the intention of inspiring hundreds, thousands and millions of people first. Anything else will come after that as if by magic.

Are you ready to write as if nobody is watching?

"Your writing genius is bursting, is shouting. Please give it a pen"

Debora Luzi

Writing PROMPTS

"The whispers will come and knock at your door for you to listen to them. The more you ignore them, the louder they will get and the more miserable you will become. LISTEN!"

Debora Luzi

Prompt 1: Purpose

Today I want to talk to you about purpose.

When we give purpose to anything we do, an action, a piece of writing, a word, it is like feeding that purpose with fuel, giving it a reason to exist and charging it with energy.

Things without a purpose do not go very far.

I want to invite you from today to ALWAYS give a purpose to anything you write for yourselves and your business......

Before you start writing STOP and ask yourself: "Why am I writing this? What is the purpose of it?" Once you get the answer set the intention and imagine sending it straight to the universe.

Some of the purposes can be:

- to let stuff out
- to get engagement
- to connect
- to find new clients
- to build trust with your followers
- to sell a certain product

From today, pay attention. Do not write for the sake of writing. Give your writing a purpose.

Take pen and paper and start this prompt with these words:

"I am writing because..."

Let the words flow, really connect to the reason why you have decided to pick up this book and show up every day with your own content.

Go deep.

Once you think you've got the reason why, keep asking why and why until you peel all the layers off this beautiful onion called purpose.

Discoverer

"Write as if no one is watching!"

Debora Luzi

Prompt 2: The Writer Inquisition

Gorgeous writers, so this week is all about finding the tone of your voice, your melody, your rhythm, your groove.

I want to help you find this through a series of questions, which you might think are not related at all.

Let's explore this.

I want you to start to get to know yourself so well and to know every single piece of you, I want you to get to know yourself upside down so that you can truly identify what is your groove and flavour and ultimately splash all of your content with it.

Reply to each question below. To make you understand the power of this exercise I have given you my answers.

Who is your favourite singer and why?

Jennifer Lopez came to mind. I like her because she can dance, sing, act and produce, so has multiple skills. She is a bit of a prima donna, bossy, aggressive but gentle. She likes to be in charge. I like to be "bossy" and direct in my writing, especially when I write sales content, I love to multitask, I love to show up, exactly how she does it.

What is your favourite song and why?

This must be 'The Greatest' by Sia. The song starts softly, to then explode and get to a beautiful crescendo. The words are super motivating, empowering. The whole song makes me think about energy, stamina, about never giving up, about resilience. My content is always full of motivation, inspiring people to never give up and keep going. My words are full of encouragement and resilience.

What is your favourite fruit and why?

Cherry, for sure. Juicy, red, small, delicious and a bit classy. The cherry on top of the cake that brings the final touch, the surprise, the final results. And funnily enough I often use the expression "This was the cherry on top of the cake" in my content. I like to deliver surprises, I like to tease my audience in my content, exactly what you would do with a cherry.

Who is the most inspiring person you know and why?

Tough one again. There are a few I can think of, including Oprah, Sylvester Stallone and J.K. Rowling. What do they have in common? They did not take no for an answer and went against everything to follow their vision. My content is full of this energy, the energy of determination to overcome the naysayers and personal demons.

Who is the singer you truly dislike and why?

Westlife. Their music is too wishy-washy. Too bland. It has no flavours. Too much drama too. I like to be direct on my content. I like to express my opinions openly and I do not like to get caught on internet drama with all its blaming and shaming and fingers pointing.

If you were a song, what song would you be, and why?

I am truly following my intuition here, Katy Perry, 'Roarrrr'..... which is not my favourite in terms of tune, but that is what my intuition tells me right now. I know why, because I feel I have an untamed lion inside of me, a limitless energy go, GO! GO! GO!

What have I learnt about myself through this questioning?

That I like to lead, that I can be bossy. I love to be direct in my writing, cheeky (like a cherry) and deliver top class content (the cherry on top). I learnt I am feisty and gentle at the same time, compassionate but not over the top as I have an urge to take people to their crescendo path in life.

Now, get inspired and write your answers. See how your answers will help you understand a bit more about yourself and your own groove and flavours.

After answering all the questions, you could start the prompt with these words:

"What I discovered about myself today is that...."

Describe the way you are and the way you like to do business. This will definitely help you build rapport with your audience and help them to connect (or not) with you.

Discoverer

Writing Mantra for today...

I love writing

Prompt 3: One day in the life of a feeling

Writing stories is becoming so trendy right now, but how many people can actually share their stories in a way that will make their audience remember them for years to come? Not many. Do you know why? Because something is missing in those stories.....FEELINGS!

Feelings help you take your audience into your personal journey so that they can connect to you at a deeper level.

Feelings help your audience to understand if you understand them and if you speak their language.

Getting to know the feelings of your soul clients is vital for you.

I have created a very beautiful exercise, which I want to share with you today, that helps me go deep within the feelings and totally FEEL THEM and UNDERSTAND THEM.

Are you ready to do the exercise?

- ✎ I want you to think about 10 feelings your soul client feels daily (for instance, frustration, sadness, loneliness, unhappiness etc)

- ✎ Now look at the list and choose 3

- ✎ Look at the list again and choose one, the most dominant and strong one

- ✎ Now close your eyes and imagine you are putting on a dress that represents that feeling. This will help you with the personification of it.

🖉 Now write a story of a typical day in the life of THIS FEELING. Ask how this feeling feels, how it responds to the external environment, what it says to itself and what its thoughts are.

Start writing and let the pen flow.

I will give you an example. I choose Frustration.

" Hi, my name is frustration. I know my master does not like me much and I stop him/her from doing so many things, but I cannot help it.

I try to leave her alone in the morning as I am quite slow to wake up and often, I need very strong reasons to get activated.

But sometimes I just need a little stimulus to activate myself. I keep quiet in the background, and I shake quite a bit. I am quiet when motivation wins over me and my master is all happy.

I know I am not liked very much. I keep quiet, but for instance, when motivation makes my master post something online, I watch silently. I really do not want to show up but then I get curious.....I nudge my master to go and check the response......and when I see there is none I start to warm up, I start to show up.....and I am all over my master and I make her freeze and feel anxious."

Did you get the gist? Now is your turn.

You cannot imagine how this will help you to articulate how your soul client feels so that you can use the right words and expressions when you speak to them with your content.

Salesperson

Prompt 4: The word blender

Let's awaken your creativity today, shall we?

I want to invite you to play a game that will help you to exercise your creative muscle because writing is about being creative and being able to write with any inspirations or stimuli and in total flow.

Take a piece of paper which you will carry around with you all day.

Start collecting words and phrases throughout the day and write them down.

Be guided by your intuition to choose the words. Do not overthink it.

For instance, your partner or child might tell you a word or you might see a sentence on the billboard while waiting for the bus or you might hear a word on the radio. Or it could be the title of a song.

Write down the ones that stand out more and at the end of the day take a look at all the words you have collected and create a story with them. It could be a short fiction story, a real story or a piece of content related to something you do or a message you want to share with your audience.

The fun and rules are that you need to use all the words, phrases, anecdotes, sentences, song titles you collected throughout the day.

Start writing, even if it makes no sense or if what you write is not perfect. Who likes perfection anyway?

What you are doing is simply igniting your creativity and ability to write in the flow.

Discoverer, Storyteller, Teacher

"When you cannot find the right words to write, go and do something you love while holding a pen in your hand"

Debora Luzi

Prompt 5: Nature of contrasts

Day & Night
Sun & Moon
Feminine & Masculine
Hot & Cold
Summer & Winter

There is so much duality in the world. And not only in the world outside of us, but in the world inside of us. Duality is just everywhere and indispensable for the existence of humanity and all things.

There would not be life if only the day would exist without the night.

There would not be harmony if only the feminine would exist without the masculine.

I want to take you on a journey to explore duality. Duality means opposition and contrast.

I want you to think of any opposing thoughts you may have regularly. Explore a part of you that is the total opposite of who you usually show you are.

Explore the duality in your business. Maybe you teach something but the result you get is the total opposite.

I want to give you some food for thought here and make you think.

When you think about the word " duality" where does your mind takes you? What are the first thoughts that come to mind?

There is an invitation also to accept each and every contrasting part of you, and in the world you live in.

We are above all everything and its exact opposite, even if you do not want to admit it or are unaware of it.

Ready to explore duality? Let's start writing.

You can start the prompt with these words....

"I am X and its exact opposite" or "Life is simply not only black or white."

Or create your very own entrance.

Discoverer, Storyteller

Writing Mantra for today...

Writing comes naturally to me

Prompt 6: Find your WORDS!

You know that standing out from the crowd is key in your business. But not standing out pretending to be someone else, but just being yourself.

I want to invite you to think about words that characterise only you, your personality, character and your business.

Let's open a "word account" and start depositing all these words that you normally use in your day-to-day conversations. These could be catchphrases, catchy hashtags, anecdotes, riddles or special words.

If you cannot think of any, I invite you to start creating your personal "word account" from now.

Let's get a pen and paper and let's start brainstorming.

This will help people to recognise you from miles away and give a "you" flavour to your writing.

Here are some of mine......

- Dare to desire
- Much daring and written love to you
- Dare to go live
- The cherry on top
- You may think that
- Wait, there is more!

- Women who dare

- Tomorrow is too late!

- Oh, you know that already!

- Let me tell you...

- You are worth it!

- Daramazing!

Daramazing!

You may wonder where this word comes from? I have taken the liberty of creating my own word, made up of two of my favourite words: *Dare* and *Amazing*.

So let's start creating and depositing those words and I challenge you to write a piece of content with all of them. You can pick any of the other prompts and write it with your word account in mind.

Discoverer, Storyteller

"Be direct! DO NOT fluff around with words. Say it as it is!"

Debora Luzi

Prompt 7: Research! FACT! Research! FACT!

I want to share a harsh truth...

> *People will believe bodies of authority*
> *more, than "normal" people.*

In fact, there have been many studies where they took a bunch of people and gave them some absurd tasks, sometimes not very ethical.

One group was given the task by a normal person. You can imagine that not many people complied with the request. But the other group was given the task by someone wearing a lab gown. Even if the task sounded unfair and out of alignment for them, a whopping 65% complied with the request.[2]

This shows you something.

People believe certain facts and will do certain things when they are told by a body of authority.

I am getting there! Wait.

So for instance, when you hear a fact that the University of Oxford has made a claim about certain research, you are more likely to believe it and trust it because it comes from a trusted institution.

So while you are building your authority in the market, you could use this to your advantage by using certain research

---

2. The experiment was conducted by Stanley Milgram (Milgram, 1963 as cited in the book *Methods of Persuasions* by Nick Kolenda)

or case studies related to your business done by established bodies or organisations.

Let me give you a few examples here:

Let's say you are a love coach.....You could share case studies by the university of X that states that 50% of people who are in a happy relationship have more success in life and tend to create bigger projects.....You share the statistic or case studies and then you introduce your opinion and ultimately your service....BOOM!

Note: make sure to pick real case studies. So, you may want to research online or buy a few magazines to educate yourself.

Let's look at another example: for instance, if you are a confidence coach you could say that The Institute of Massachusetts (I am inventing here for the purpose of this prompt) found that very confident people live longer and had less heart disease etc...you explain the fact, you give your input (this is very important in order to make it personal to you and to show that you know about the subject too), then you propose your offer. This is a great way of showing your authority by using those of other organisations.

So, are you ready to try it? Let's start with finding some case studies. If you look, they are everywhere, just pick up a newspaper or a magazine. I am so excited to see what you will develop with this.

Teacher, Salesperson

Prompt 8: Goodbye!

Today's prompt might seem a bit sad at first but trust me it will be an eye-opening exercise for you and for your content writing.

I want you to write a letter.

This is the scenario:

You are dead and you are in front of the universal gates to enter the other world. Your life has ended.

Before you enter the gate, you notice a beautiful chair with a small table. You get closer and on the small table, you find a pen and some paper. You grab a piece of paper and you read:

"Before you go, write a letter to yourself thanking yourself for the life you lived. Was your life how you wished it to be? Do you have any regrets? Open yourself up and be true to yourself. Is there anything you would have done differently?"

Sit down, grab the pen and start writing.

This exercise is so powerful as it will serve you for two reasons:

1. To give you some strong motivation in case you realize that you are still not living the life you desire or doing the things that set your heart on fire

2. To understand your soul client better and the emotional triggers that will make them take action. You can write this letter as if you were your soul

client. Imagine he/she is dead, and he/she is in front of the gate writing this letter. What would they write in that letter?

What regrets will they have? Then you can use this content (especially the regrets, the things not done) to write a powerful piece of content to "wake them up" and take action.

Storyteller, Salesperson

Writing Mantra for today...

Words flow through me with
ease and joy

Prompt 9: Once upon a child

Let's go back in time today.

The prompt for today is to write freestyle about your most beautiful and memorable childhood memory.

Recall the facts, the memories, the expressions on people's faces, the ones on your face. The emotions you experienced, the landscapes around you, the colours. Be as descriptive as possible.

Imagine yourself living that experience again through your writing and let the readers be immersed in your words.

The memory could be a particular moment in your child lifeline where you experienced something that significantly changed you, or where you experienced much joy or any memory that you can link to who you are today or why you do what you do.

I want to invite you to think about how you can use this piece of writing. Before you do, consider whether there is a lesson you have learnt from the story, a message you want to deliver to your audience, and if there is, make sure you add that at the end of your writing.

Try to bring the reader with you while you tell the story. Maybe ask questions like "Have you ever felt like that?" or "Has this ever happened to you?" or "What would you have done if you were me?"

These simple questions could really help you in engaging your reader more and make them feel part of the story.

You can start the prompt with these words...

"I can relive that moment as if it was now"

Or simply start with your own sentence. Remember, do not use "When I was child..." or "20 years ago..." make it more interesting. Remember the heading is crucial to make your readers stop by.

Storyteller

"Words are your most powerful marketing tools"

Debora Luzi

Prompt 10: Dear Solution

How easy would it be to sell to your clients if you knew exactly the benefits that your products and services will bring to them? So much easier. Do you know why? Because they will know EXACTLY what the benefits of buying are. So, let's write about this today in a different way.

You receive a letter from someone you have not heard from in a long while.

Surprised, you open the letter and you start reading....

So much has changed in their life and so much has happened. They are in a very challenging situation right now. As you read, you realise that you can totally help this person, that you hold the key to their happiness. That you have the solution to their problem.

You grab a pen and paper and you decide to write them a letter, telling them *how* you can help them, without mentioning what you do, without giving yourself any titles or job titles.

Write from your heart, write as if the life of this person depends on you and on every single word you write. Make this a life or death situation. Explain all the benefits of working with you.

Do not focus on *what* you will do together, focus on the solutions you will bring them.

How will they feel after working with you?

How will their situation change?

Go wild, no worries about writing the wrong or the right things. If your HEART leads, EVERYTHING you write will be just perfect.

For those of you that want the beginning line, this could be...

'Dear X, I can imagine how you feel....'

Storyteller, Salesperson

....
....
....
....
....
....
....
....
....
....
....
....
....
....
....
....
....
....
....
....

Prompt 11: Curiosity killed the cat

There are two factors that will make reading your content very interesting and engaging in the eyes and ears of your audience: Curiosity and Humour.

Even without realising it, I always inject a big dose of humour and curiosity into my content.

I do so naturally as I like to tease my readers and keep them on their toes. Not only because I want them to keep reading, but also because I want to activate their brain and make them active readers and not passive readers.

By active reader I mean the reader who is fully engaged, who hangs on every word and who is totally engrossed in the content and not easily distracted by it.

I love to add a bit of curiosity at the beginning of my content, by writing titles or sentences which will leave my audience curious to know more.

I have never been a fan of starting a piece of content with words such as "Good morning", or "here are my thoughts for the day" or.....These are simple statements and do not ignite any emotions or generate any sort of adrenaline in your reader.

Let me give you some examples here. So, these types of titles inspire curiosity as you are not giving away much.

"The three fundamental business strategies I learned from my morning walk" instead of... "While walking this morning I learnt that..."

"How to become effective at.....in one simple step..."

"A mistake you do not want to make which cost my business £X..."

Or...

"As I went to grab my running shoes this morning, I noticed something very unusual."

Do you get the gist?

Our mind is naturally curious, we are creatures that want to know everything and when we do not know something, our brain will find all the ways to get that answer.

So today let's leave your audience wanting more...

Write a story starting with any of the headlines I gave above as an example.

Remember to not create curiosity and then give it all away in the next few lines. Keep the "secret" alive for as long as you can.

Storyteller, Teacher

Writing Mantra for today...

I am a confident writer

Prompt 12: Doctor's prescription

Let's become very creative and inject a bit of excitement into these "too much talked about" pain points your clients feel, and to the solutions that you bring to ease or eliminate the pain altogether.

I am sure you've heard so much about pain and solutions and sometimes you may feel you've had enough of talking about them and hearing about them.

I know! However, these are paramount if you want to clearly communicate your message to your potential clients.

Imagine you are a doctor today and that your client/patient comes to you with their pain.

I want you to imagine examining them and asking them questions and eventually writing a prescription for them, in the same way a doctor would prescribe you rest, lots of water, walks in the park and St. John's Wort if your symptoms are headache and stress.

So, let's play today. I want to invite you to write a detailed prescription to your client who comes to you for that particular pain you can magically alleviate.

Be creative, look outside the box.

Maybe you can recommend a herb, an exercise, a meditation, a routine, a formula, an action to take or anything that will help your client to alleviate their pain.

This exercise will help you to become clearer about what solutions you bring and also to possibly add a few "ingredients" to your "solution medicine cabinet".

Remember your client is in pain and they come for a fast solution.

So, what would you prescribe them?

And let's see where this piece of writing might take you as always.

Teacher, Salesperson

"Let your WORDS flow and your INTUITION glow!"

Debora Luzi

Prompt 13: Houmous anyone? Oops I meant humour...

I mentioned in prompt 11 that the two most important factors when it comes to writing and engaging your audience are curiosity and humour. Today I want to explore the humour part.

Adding humour to your stories, your content and your marketing is important so as to assure a great engagement. It is important that you make your audience smile and feel good from time to time. You want them to feel good when they think of you.

Shall we write some humour today?

Write about the time when you learned a big life lesson and tell it with humour. Make your audience laugh and really hold their breath.

Maybe you remember the time when you forgot someone's name and you thought you were talking to someone else or that time when your teacher caught you copying an exam paper?

Remember that writing for your business is providing your audience with a variety of content and stories, much of which will need to be entertaining.

You can start the prompt with.... "I never felt so embarrassed before like on that day..."

Or "Everyone started laughing..."

Storyteller

Prompt 14: A visit in space

Spacing is so important when it comes to writing content, especially on social media. People on social media are after quick, short and satisfying content.

Let's be real. Aren't you put off by a post that is so long and has no space between each paragraph?

I personally am.

And actually, I do not read these posts even though they might have the best content ever.

So, let's go back to all the content you have written recently and check how you have been doing with spacing.

Are

you

generous

with

spacing

or

do

you

write

all

in

one

big

chunk?

For instance, I always leave a couple of spaces between the title/headline of my post and the actual content.

Often, I write the points I want to make in different lines, or I separate the direct speeches.

This will help the reader to stay more engaged and read with more flow.

Let's experiment today. Go back to one of the prompts you have written so far or write a new one and make sure you are very "space-conscious". Be very generous and notice the difference this will make.

Another idea to use this prompt is to ask your audience a question such as "what do you think about long content or content that is written all in one big chunk? Do you prefer it or hate it?"

This could start a great conversation and engagement on your profile.

Another idea is that you could express your view on this first and then ask the question in the end.

Discoverer, Storyteller, Teacher, Leader, Salesperson

Writing Mantra for today...

I write as if no one is watching

Prompt 15: Dear Me

I would love you to write a letter to yourself thanking yourself for all the things you have achieved, all the mistakes you have made, and all the great lessons you have learned.

Be as descriptive as possible, honour yourself, go creative and write, write, write as if you are seeing yourself from the top, simply observing.

Imagine that you write from your higher self, thanking the 'You" that was living and managing your life.

We are simply not used to talking about how great we are, or all the successes we have achieved. Today give yourself permission to do that. Boast about your achievements, your results and how great you are.

And get used to doing it often. Remember, the more you shine the more you invite others to do the same.

You can start the prompt with these words:

"Thank you...(insert your name)".

Discoverer, Storyteller.

"When you talk about the results you deliver make sure your audience can SEE, FEEL and TASTE them"

Debora Luzi

Prompt 16: Clearance of words and energy

When I started my business, I used to offer healing sessions using different healing modalities such as Reiki, Theta Healing®, Crystal Healing and coaching.

Part of the healing I used to do consisted of releasing stagnant energy in the different chakras or points of energy in our body in order to provide more balance, wellness and harmony in people's everyday lives.

One of the exercises I used to give my clients to clear their throat chakra's energy was to think of a person in their life with whom they had not spoken their truth, for fear of hurting their feelings or not being liked.

Often a 'blocked throat chakra' means that someone struggles to speak their truth and saying "no" to people and that they have lots of words inside them that have not been *fully* expressed.

I am inviting you to write a letter to someone you know you have unresolved "words issues" with, which means that you have not told her/him how you really felt about a certain behaviour or situation.

In simple words, speak your truth, tell them how you really feel about it, get those words out, anger frustration, sadness, happiness, let them all out.

This prompt is not only useful for you to create some storytelling content but also to clear some stagnant energy around your throat chakra. When you finish writing, read the post out loud (not in front of a mirror), perhaps out in nature or somewhere where the energy can flow easily and share it with your audience.

When you share it, make sure you share the learnings and the lessons and what speaking your truth has given you.

After writing the letter you can start the prompt with these words:

"I did not realise how resentful I have been"

Or

"This is what I learnt from forgiving"

Storyteller

Prompt 17: Business in love

I am in a very loving mood today so I thought I would do something fun and related to love. I will not ask you to write a love letter to your loved ones or to yourself, but to your business.

I have done this several times and I cannot tell you how many "aha" moments I got from doing this exercise.

I want you to really put yourself in the shoes of your business and write a love letter to it.

As always do not think about it too much.

🖉 Let your imagination guide you

🖉 Let your intuition inspire you

🖉 Let your words move you

🖉 Keep writing, keep writing, keep writing

Start the prompt with these words:

"Dear Business (the name of your Business) ..."

Your business might love this so much and it might have some secrets to tell you.

You may want to write reflections and ideas you get from writing this letter and share it with your audience.

Discoverer, Salesperson

Writing Mantra for today...

My message is clear and
to the point

Prompt 18: My shoes are too big

Today I would like you to get into your client's shoes and live their life for a few moments or a full day.

I want you to particularly focus on what their routine is, and how they are feeling throughout the day.

This exercise will help you to understand the different emotions they go through during the day.

So, for instance, take into consideration a normal day in the life of your soul client from the moment they wake up to the moment they fall asleep.

This exercise is *magic*, as it helps you to really understand your soul client better and to find out some of the language you can use to attract them in your marketing.

Start writing:

I... as if you were the client and describe the routines and the feelings.

"I wake up at 6 am feeling already tired as I did not get much sleep last night. I had another argument with my husband. I feel he does not get me at all. We are getting to the final straw.

I somehow manage to find strength and take the children to school. But I get really frustrated when I see all the other mothers happily smiling while all I feel inside is exhaustion.

My children want to play with me, and I still have so much to do as I could not focus the whole morning" etc.

Another example...

"I love mornings. I wake up so early to do my daily routine to somehow alleviate the feelings of anxiety that I have since starting my business and seeing all those bills on my coffee table.

I drop the children at school and all I can think of is 'where will my next client come from'..." etc, etc.

Why do we do this exercise?

Because once you write this and become aware of your client's routine and the emotions, she/he feels throughout the day, you can use it to write powerful and effective marketing content with a specific audience in mind and using specific, targeted language.

Let me show you the power of writing with very specific language.

Imagine you start a piece of content like this:

"Are you feeling stressed? Fed up?

Do you feel exhausted and do you say to yourself that you cannot do this anymore?"

(A very general statement that does not go deep into HOW your soul client FEELS)

Let's try this statement instead taken from your client's daily routine:

"Have you just dropped the children at school and as you wave them goodbye, you start feeling that sense of anxiety in your stomach?

The thoughts of sitting at your desk and thinking where your next client will come from, overwhelm you..."

Can you see the difference? The second statement is far more powerful, and it will help your audience to identify with it thinking that you have written that content just for them.

So have a go now. Be very specific. Take some time to close your eyes and see your soul client's life from above as an observer, from the morning to the time they close their eyes.

I am a big fan of specific language and I hope you will become one too. Your soul client will love it too.

Salesperson

"Before you tell your audience what you do, tell them who you are."

Debora Luzi

Prompt 19: I brag, and you?

In a previous prompt, I asked you to brag about your achievements and today I will ask you to brag through the words of your client.

We can brag about how good we are all day long, but there is nothing more credible to the eyes of your reader than someone else bragging about you and your services. This builds instant trust in you and your business.

I know that it can feel too "braggy" or "pretentious" to go out there and share the amazing results you get with your clients. I know it because this is exactly how I felt at the beginning of my entrepreneurial journey. I was terrified of doing it and I had a constant voice telling me "Who are you to share this, Debora?"

"Who am I not?" I replied one day and started bragging a bit more.

I always encourage my clients and my audience to share any results their clients achieve, whether small, medium, big or extra-large. Any size matters.

I had a very bad experience with sharing a client testimonial once. I asked permission but then it all went pear-shaped as the client had only wanted it to be shared with a few chosen people and not everyone. This incident kept me on the hide for a long time, but then I started to slowly regain confidence and my clients were sharing results without me having to ask.

Always ask or write the result in a general way without mentioning any names or ask permission to share.

Your prompt for today is to share a testimonial from your client.

Do not simply share it, create a story around this person, and make sure you say:

HOW she/he was BEFORE working with you

HOW she/he is now AFTER working with you

Make sure you ALWAYS mention the TRANSFORMATIONS they went through.

If you do not have any testimonials right now, write about your ideal testimonials. What testimonial would you like to receive?

> 🖊 What is the client saying about you?

> 🖊 What are the transformations she/he had after working with you?

> 🖊 How does she feel now?

> 🖊 How is she going to rave about you to her friends and family....

Go wild. Write whatever comes to your mind. Let the words come out unfiltered.

This is *your* shiny moment.

Leader

Prompt 20: Around the world in 80 days

When I was younger, I always had this dream of writing a book about my travelling.

I visited more than 55 countries and I had some amazing, daring adventures. I mainly travelled on a budget as a backpacker and often, I worked to get money to get to the next country.

I often talk about countries I have seen or experiences I lived in my content. In a recent piece of content, I shared a story of me travelling in South America and the amazing transformations that happened in me during this time. The content received so much engagement.

The content shared some of my travelling stories, and the story of a very difficult situation I was in, both physical and emotional. It was deep, and I shared my feelings in a very open way.

I want to invite you today to go back in time and think about a travelling experience you had that was:

    🖊 funny   🖊 adventurous

    🖊 amusing   🖊 eye-opening

    🖊 life-changing   🖊 relaxing

    🖊 curious

Tell the story. Tell about the people, the colours, the different cultures, the emotions you felt and remember to always deliver a message at the end.

The message is usually the reason why you are telling that particular story. Do you want to make your readers laugh, or do you want to give them a piece of advice or do you simply want to entertain them with the story?

Try to *not* start the story with "5 years ago I went travelling to......."

Move away from these types of beginnings. These are good for books or long writing but not for short content, where you need to catch people's attention.

You can start with a sentence such as "I was so scared....", "that was the best day of my life..." or " I never thought this country would teach me so much...

One little tip here. When you start with these kinds of sentences do not give away the rest of the story in the next paragraphs. Keep your audience waiting for it and wanting more. Show them the cherry, and as they think they go to bite it, you take it away and keep going.

Storyteller

Writing Mantra for today...

My audience loves my content

Prompt 21: Eat me!

I am a big fan of making my reader see, feel, smell, taste and touch my words through engaging the 5 senses when I produce content. Today I want to help you explore the sense of taste in your writing.

I am such a big fan of great food and recently I was reminded of the importance of being present when tasting things and using your mouth.

I participated in a beautiful Forest Bathing session[3] with Deborah Mendes which awakened all of my senses.

I was given an exercise where I had to eat a strawberry really, really slow.

A strawberry never tasted so delicious like that day. I even did not realise that I could actually feel the taste of those little black dots on the strawberry.

I never realised that tasting a strawberry would send signals of joy and excitement to my brain.

Why don't you all go and try this and then come here and write about it?

✎ Make sure you are not disturbed

✎ Pick a piece of fruit you absolutely love

✎ Start looking at it

---

3. Japanese method of relaxation amongst trees and nature.

🖋 Visualise yourself eating it

🖋 Start eating it SLOWLY, so slow like a turtle running a race.

🖋 Close your eyes

🖋 Make sure you engage the tongue, the teeth, chew it slowly and deeply. Then write about your experience.

Let's practise this even further. I want to invite you to write a story. Tell the story of how you started to work for yourself. How did it happen?

Add to the story "tasty words" and "tasty metaphors".

Here are some examples:

"It was as bitter as a lemon"

"I felt squashed like a tomato in a tin"

"I was as excited as a child sticking his tongue into a gigantic ice cream"

"The idea was so inviting like a mouth-watering tiramisu standing in front of you"

I guarantee that your readers will be more likely to remember the story when you engage their sense of taste and next time, they eat something you have described, they will think of you and your story.

You could also explore the story using the sense of smell. Some examples could be: "It smelled as bad as a fish left on a plate for a week."

Storyteller

"I do not follow, I lead. You are a leader even if all you lead is yourself"

Debora Luzi

Prompt 22: CTA...no I am not a cat spelt the wrong way!

Let's talk CTA (Call to Action).

It is very important that you get used to adding a call to action to your content. If you don't, your readers may not realise that you are in business and that you are actually selling.

A call to action, as the words say, is a set of instructions where you invite your audience to buy your products and services or to take any action that could simply be to answer a question or follow your social media account.

There is not a particular formula to write a call to action. I like to create them out of anything, however I would like to give you some guidelines to follow if you want to write effective CTAs.

I want you to consider that one piece of content with a CTA is not enough for you to sell your products and services. It is important that you habituate your audience to take actions in your content.

Let's follow a simple structure to create a sales post with a CTA.

1. Choose one product or service you want to sell. Write down the clear benefits of the product. How will it help the buyer? How will their life change once they buy this product? What are the visible and tangible results of buying this product?

    How will they feel afterwards? Please be specific. Do not simply say they will feel more empowered or more confident. Explain how they will see they are more confident, how will their life change after being more confident. (I am just giving an example with being more confident as the solution). How will they act differently? Will they finally apply to speak at that big conference? Will they finally look in the mirror and fall in love with what they see?

2. Start the content with either a catchy phrase, a sentence or a statement which identifies the solution to the problem you solve: Examples:

"I got 5 clients in a week."

"I made £1,000 in 2 days."

"Mary, my client, stopped taking antidepressants for the first time." etc......

"How would you feel if you were to sign up two clients with ease this week?" Or "...if you were to stop waking up in the middle of the night and sleep like a baby?". You need to add the solution you bring for instance more clients, more confidence, more sleeps etc.

3. Introduce the solution. Write the name of the product or service you want to sell. Avoid saying one coaching session, or an hour consultation. Give the session, program or product a SPECIFIC name which possibly contains the end result people will sign up to. Examples:

"10k in 10 days."

"From Content to Cash" – this is the title of my famous free 5 days writing challenge

"From unnoticed to popular in 31 days."

4. State who this product is for. Examples:

"For you who have no idea what content to put out there"

"For you who finds writing daily content exhausting and wishes there was a magic wand to create content on steroids"

These are some of the sentences I would use for my particular field.

5. Write the SPECIFIC benefits you have identified in point 1 above.

6. Write a CLEAR CTA, with direct words, talking about the sale, not asking for it. Give your reader clear instructions on how to sign up for the offer, where to click, and what to expect after clicking.

7. End the content with a motivational quote, an uplifting push that will give them "permission" to buy this product. Examples:

"You deserve it!"

"Your clients are waiting for you! It is time you filled up your tank!"

These are just examples. There are so many different ways to write sales content with a CTA. This is a good practice to start with.

You could also invite your audience to comply with a smaller CTA where you do not ask them to buy something but simply to follow you, like your business page or give you an opinion on something.

Once you have had a go at writing it, put it out there straight away and start getting used to doing that very often.

Salesperson

Prompt 23: The poet in you!

Have you ever written a poem?

Have you ever fallen in love with a poem or has anyone written a poem to you?

I am going to an event tonight where the focus is on personal empowerment poetry. So I thought it would be a great idea to get those poems out, start to share them and most of all to use them to create some great content for my audience.

I remember writing poems when I was a child. I wrote a few poems to this guy that I really loved and others around solitude and sadness. What about you?

Can you dig some of them out? Maybe you can use them to enrich a story you are going to tell...Or maybe you can write a new one about a particular emotion you feel right now...

Maybe you could write one about the sky, moon, or about a person you deeply love. Let's get creative and start writing.

You could use your poems in many ways in your content. Let's explore a few:

- ✐ use it to start a story

- ✐ share it in your community to inspire and motivate

- ✐ invite people to share their poems

- ✐ ask a question about poems.... what is your favourite poem and why or...have you ever written a poem, to whom?

📎 share it to enrich your content

📎 use a certain poem to introduce some teachings or give value about something

Ready? Let's have a go.

The sky is the limit. Time to unleash the poet in you.

Discoverer, Teacher, Leader

Writing Mantra for today...

I sell with ease and joy
through my content

Prompt 24: Let me watch some soap!

I got inspired to write this prompt by a soap opera I watched recently called *Sin Teta si Hay Paraíso*, translated from the Spanish language "There is paradise even without breasts"!

I never watch soap operas, apart from when I was a child as my mum was watching a few of them, *Dallas*, anyone, or *The Bold and The Beautiful*?

But the other night my husband was scrolling through Netflix and noticed there was this Colombian series. I sat down to keep him company and I was hooked within minutes.

One night I even stayed up until 4 am to watch it.

Thank goodness I realised that the soap opera had over 200 episodes, so I decided to give up on it on the spot.

The whole experience gave me some food for thought about why people love soap operas so much.

The answer is because of something I teach all the time and I actually use in my writing and videos a lot:

Suspense.

The dictionary explains it like this:

"a state or feeling of excited or anxious uncertainty about what may happen"

BOOM!

People have a natural tendency to want to know more, to want to know the end, to want to know what will happen. Their curiosity will take them to unimaginable places.

How many times have you gone the extra mile because you wanted to know "what happens next?"

How can you recreate this type of soap opera suspense in your writing?

There are so many ways you can do this and the reason why you want to do it is to make your audience come back to your content, website, social media account etc.

I want you to think about a story or something that happened to you, which was curious or unusual. Actually, any stories can work here. And even the most boring story, broken down into two or more pieces, can become 'attractive" because of this "I want to know more" factor.

After you've got a story, break it down into two or three pieces (I would not recommend more than this for now).

Start writing the first chunk. Then post it on social media, (or you can do a blog part 1 and part 2) or even an article.....You could write the title of the story and let people know that this is PART 1 or at the bottom, you can say: "to be continued" or "watch out for the next piece".

These are just examples, think of how you can let your audience know that this is 2/3 part of a story. (you could use this structure for training as well, for instance, "the three secrets to....." and every day you share one secret etc).

Have fun with this. What story will you create that will keep your readers dying to know more and coming back to your content?

Discoverer, Storyteller, Leader

"Always be your first and loudest number one fan"

Debora Luzi

Prompt 25: The power of consequences

CAUSE and EFFECT (consequences).....

Today I want to focus your attention on the power of consequences and to the fact that it is vital that you talk about "consequences" in your content.

Let me explain.

We are clear on the importance of knowing EXACTLY what the problem is you are solving, and consequently the solution you are bringing to solve this problem.

The problem you solve and the solution you bring is in reality only the surface of what you do and what you can offer.

I want to invite you to go deeper and start using the REAL reasons, or consequences to the problem so that your audience can connect more to it and understand that what you offer is exactly what they need!

Let me give you some examples here to make you understand.

Here are some examples of a problem you may solve:

- help people to get to their ideal weight (remember it is better to say ideal weight than lose weight)

- help people to make more money

- help people to find the love of their life

- help people to overcome depression or anxiety

These are solutions that you may address in your marketing.

Let's think about WHAT CONSEQUENCES these problems may cause if they are not resolved.

For instance, let's take the problem of finding the love of their life.

I want you to think what the CONSEQUENCES of not finding the love of their life are.

These are some examples:

🖉 always go on holiday alone

🖉 feeling really depressed when all your friends show up with their partner

🖉 feeling unloved and finding comfort in chocolate

🖉 feeling ugly and giving up on going out and meeting new people....

So, these are some examples of the consequences of not finding love. It is VITAL that you market these consequences and not only the problem on the surface.

For instance, the CONSEQUENCES of not making enough money could be:

🖉 constantly arguing with your partner

🖉 feeling a failure

🖉 saying no to friends when they invite you to go out for dinner

🖉 stopping the gym membership or the monthly visit to the hairdresser etc....

Are you ready to explore this?

Think of the problem you solve and the solution you bring.

Now think of the consequences in your soul client's life of not having that solution YET. How their life looks, what decisions are they making instead?

🖉 Make a list and write some content with these consequences.

🖉 Add them to your marketing material and sales page.

🖉 Be as specific as possible

BOOM! Your soul client will resonate more with these examples than the usual "do you want to lose weight?"

Remember, the more you enter your soul client's mind, the more you are aware of their thinking, the better they will see you as the one ready to deliver their solution to them.

You could start the prompt like this:

"What will truly happen if you do not find the love of your life?"

or "What will truly happen if you do not get any clients this month?"

Salesperson

Prompt 26: Causes

In the previous prompt I have covered the first part of something so important I teach when it comes to attracting your soul client:

Understanding the consequences of not solving your client's problem, in deep details.

Now, let's look at the other side of the coin: the cause of the problem.

Why is it so important to look at the causes of not taking action, and finding the solution that your clients desire?

In other words, you can ask "How did they get there, WHY? In which moment, what were they doing wrong"?

When you know the CAUSES of WHY your soul client is where she/he is, you can use it in your messaging, sale pages, posts to make them understand that you know exactly why they are where they are, even if they deny it. Maybe you have been there yourself, and if you know it you can certainly help them get out of it. Knowing something means you are halfway to getting out of it.

Be daring and courageous to say exactly HOW IT IS, and to talk about the REAL causes that your clients often do not see.

Let me give you some examples.

Let's imagine that the problem of your soul client is "Not getting clients online"

The consequences of not getting clients are for instance:

- getting frustrated with their children, shouting at them
- worrying too much and having to go to therapy to calm down
- considering going back to work
- anxiety around opening the bills etc

Now, what might the causes be?

Your soul client might think that these are the obvious causes:

- too much competition
- people are not interested
- people simply do not buy
- I am not good at selling

But there are some real, deeper causes that your client may not see, or pretend not to see. Here are some examples:

- not being clear on their message. A vague message that does not talk to anyone in particular but to too many people
- worrying about what people are saying, so not showing up, selling enough
- not having their personal profile optimized as the first point of contact on social media
- following too many coaches, ideas, concepts

🖋 not investing in the right help, grabbing all the freebie
   stuff

Did you get the GIST?

This will massively help you to create the right content and
the right message.

Explore all the causes and you could have fun creating a piece
of content with each one of them.

You could start writing with these words in mind....

"You think that you are not...(the problem, getting client, or
find love etc) because.... (obvious causes)...think again!"

These are the real reasons.

Salesperson

Writing Mantra for today...

I always know what
to write next

Prompt 27: Happy Birthday to you!

Today's prompt will be short, sweet and to the point.

I absolutely love this, and I applied it with great success in the past. You get to experiment with it and as always add your personal touch and twist.

This week is my Birthday Week. My birthday is on Sunday the 25th of August.

Doing promotions or asking people to do something on your birthday is the perfect time to have the request complied with.

You might see people putting out their special offers and special deals or simply asking people to like their page or share something on their birthday.

Why would they do that? Because people absolutely love to celebrate and honour each other on their birthday.

Let's face it. Are you not "nicer" to someone just because it is their birthday? Or are you willing to forget about some grudge you may hold towards someone because it is their birthday or their special occasion?

I am sure you are.

People tend to want to please and comply with requests when there is a celebration behind it.

Think of why people raise money on their birthday instead of any other day.

I experimented with this a while back. I put a picture of me blowing out candles on social media and asked people to like my Facebook Business page. As a response, I had more likes on that day, more than any other time I asked. And let me tell you, that day it was not my birthday!

You may ask, how can I use this?

You can ask your audience to take simple actions, such as like my page, share my event, join my group or even buy a product or offer.

You can do a birthday week promotion, and have it run for the whole week.

You can use this "excuse" not only when is your birthday, but when it is your anniversary or name day or any celebration you may think of.

So, are you ready to experiment? If your birthday has already gone maybe you can think of another special day coming up.

You can start the prompt with:

"As a special gift to you on my birthday week"

Or

"I am so excited this week is my birthday week....."

Keep this type of content short and sweet and to the point.

Salesperson

"Give life to your desires and feelings. Shape them into words"

Debora Luzi

Prompt 28: Grumpy mirror

From the series "PERSUASIONS FROM THE SOUL"

Why from the soul? Because persuasion is a positive thing, a way to show that you care for your audience and your prospective clients.

These persuasion principles will help you to challenge your audience's mind and awaken them to the possibility of "what it could be like if they finally solve their problem"...

Let's call this persuasion prompt "the grumpy mirror".

Let's start by explaining this:

You might have heard of this exercise where you write down all the negative things going on in your life or all the complaints you want to make towards a person close to you (for instance your partner, child, friend, wife or husband).

Then you make the other person read your letter of complaints as if it was his or hers.

THIS creates a massive shift in the reader's point of view and point of feeling that often while reading the feelings of the other person out loud, they will understand for the first time how the person feels and go to the extreme of wanting to find a solution.

Humans, in general, tend to want to find solutions every time someone does not feel well. Think of when you go and see a friend. She/he tells you some of the challenges she/he is going through. You naturally try to comfort her, and find a solution...relax, do more of this or that...etc.

Now, let's combine the above scenarios.

When it comes to motivating someone to do something, you probably think that the best way is to say "Come on, do it" and state all the positive outcomes that they could receive from doing a particular thing (in this case it could be to join your challenge, program, event etc),

Yes, great!

But.....

There is another very powerful way which is done by mirroring back the 'down and negative' feelings of the person you want to motivate.

This has got much psychology behind it, but for now, let's explore just what is relevant for you and your writing.

When you mirror back the words and negative expression of someone reluctant to do something, it creates a sense of "awakening and awareness" to what the reality is, that the person almost wants to run away from it, deny it or find a solution.

Let me break this down for you.

Imagine you are speaking to a friend who is going through a really tough time.

You go and visit her/him and try to comfort them, telling them that life is beautiful and that there is so much waiting for them.

They reply, defeated, by telling you that life is terrible, it is not worth it and that there is nothing they can do.

Instead of convincing them otherwise, you mirror their language back at them.

You say that yes, life is terrible, that there is no point in trying as nothing will work. The best solution is to give up. Your friend will respond to this in a shocked way. After hearing their own words from someone else they will want to convince you that this is not true because of humans' natural instinct of helping and rescuing others.

They will start to uplift and suggest things they could do instead to feel better.

INCREDIBLE right?

YES! This is called reverse psychology and it is so powerful.

If you pay attention, you see this type of reaction in many situations. I use this principle with my children when they tell me they cannot do something, or that the world is unfair.

As soon as I say: "You are right" this creates a shift in their mind, they do not expect it and they will start to "convince" me that the opposite is true.

You get the gist of this? Why don't you go and explore this principle and see how you can incorporate it in your copy to persuade people?

You could start the prompt with these words: "I hear you, what is the point of solving your problem or even spending time and resources to solve it?"

Let's see where this will take you and how you can use this piece of writing in your marketing.

Leader, Salesperson

Writing Mantra for today...

I trust my intuition and my
heart to deliver the right
words to me

Prompt 29: Bang!

Writing for your business and writing to engage your audience often is NOT about the techniques and the tricks...but about creativity and imagination.

This prompt will help you to switch on your creativity light and ignite the storyteller in you.

Write a story starting from this:

"As I am sitting on my sofa, I hear a knock on the door. Surprised, I stand up and walk to the door thinking: "I am not expecting anybody today. I have not left the house for a week and I have not arranged for any visit."

I keep walking, and I hear another knock, this time much louder.

I finally get to the door and as I open it..."

What happened...?????

Let your imagination run wild and write the rest of the story.

And see how you can be more creative in your content today.

Storyteller

"Comparing your writing to those of others betrays your intuition"

Debora Luzi

Prompt 30: If... I would...

Just write anything that comes to your mind after this:

"If I had no fear of showing up as I am, I would..."

Just let it out. Really imagine what you would do if you had the courage to show up raw, real, authentic all the time. If you had no fear of being criticized and judged.

- What would you write about?
- What would you say?
- How would you show up?
- How differently would you behave online?

Let's explore and get intimate with your fears.

Maybe you can use this piece of content to tell a story to your audience of how you have overcome your biggest fear or how you are about to overcome it.

You could start the prompt with these words:

"I once had a fear..."

Storyteller, Leader

Prompt 31: Light that fire!

I have been so excited about the whole idea of the first Women Who Dare to Desire Conference that I wanted to share and explore the excitement with you.

Let me start by saying that EXCITEMENT is very contagious if done in the right way and is great in order to get great engagement.

I have so many people coming to me and tell me that they love following me because I always seem passionate and excited about what I do.

Sharing your excitement with your audience is an absolutely wonderful thing that will motivate and inspire them.

Now I am not talking about doing this every single day. I am a big advocate of giving your audience a variety of content, something I teach in all my training in The Writing Academy for Entrepreneurs.

I want to give you a few tips about sharing your excitement:

- always give a deep reason for your excitement, do not just say... "I am so excited about launching my new program, the book" etc...this is too flat and lifeless. Use other similar words. Build up to the excitement, give suspense and add curiosity.

- add stories and conversations related to your excitement

🖊 maybe ask people to guess what you are excited about

🖊 give a detailed description of how your excitement
FEELS, something like "I feel like a bottle of champagne,
being ready to open after 100 years of waiting to pop!"
Or any similar similes.

🖊 make sure you always involve your audience and make
them feel part of your excitement, by asking questions
or asking if they ever felt like that or when was the last
time they felt like that etc, etc.

Now let's start by sharing a story of excitement. Do not worry
about how you write it, for now, connect with it, give details
and focus on the feelings.

Here are some ideas on how to use this prompt. Do you have
any new offerings, ideas you have just given birth to? If yes,
share your excitement with your audience. Give details of the
situation and the offering without giving too much away.

Remember that it is more important and "exciting" to share
the beginning of a new idea and offering and "the journey
to create it" than presenting your audience with the final
already packaged offering. Let your audience almost feel as if
they are part of the project.

When I launched The Women Who Dare to Desire
Conference, I did not do it as most people do it. I did not write
a piece of content or a sale content when the conference idea
was ready, the venue booked, the ticket page live and all the
details already confirmed.

I shared every single step of the way with my audience. From
the moment I had a strong disappointment and frustration

from a refusal to speak to the moment I woke up with an idea in mind. I shared how I felt throughout, I shared my doubts, my excitement in finding the right venue, the right entertainers and the excitement each time I sold tickets.

I strongly believe that this "sharing the excitement" made the conference such a big success from day one.

Some examples of how you can start the prompt:

"I can hardly contain my excitement!"

Or "Guess why I am feeling like a bottle of champagne ready to pop?"

Storyteller, Salesperson

Writing Mantra for today...

I am a creative writer

Prompt 32: Move!

Today I want to move you from A to B or simply move you somewhere.

Think of something, a story or an experience that has had a big impact on you. What I mean by impact is that it created deep feelings, emotions, a reaction that you will remember for many years to come.

Imagine if you could move your audience to such an extent that they will remember you for a long time and associate a certain feeling/emotion/situation with you?

It is important that you occupy your audience's mind with a thought or two.

So let's look at two ways you can MOVE your audience:

The first one is by sharing a story that has really changed you. A particular story where you have experienced specific strong feelings that made you go through any kind of transformation.

In order to move the reader, it is important that you focus on how you felt, the sensations, the changes, the before and after. It is not so important here to share the whole story and the whole "she said, he said". I often see people sharing too much of their stories, confusing their audience and not going deep.

Go back in time and think of which story you could share. I often share moving stories, and I often have the validation that they truly moved people and helped me occupy that space in people's brains. So many times, people tell me they remember my story of the mountain, or the incident of my son or the story of the spelling mistake on my t-shirt "woman who dare to desire". I even had people stopping me and asking me.... are you the lady of the t-shirt story?

If you want to find out about the story you may want to go and explore my social media feeds, I often share it!

You could start the prompt like this: "I had never been moved so much in all of my life".

The second way is by telling another personal story that has moved YOU. And here when I talk about other people's stories I mean also movies, books, real-life stories I've heard.

You can tell the story and describe how it moved you, what it taught you and what your interpretation of it is. Let me give you an example here.

Let's say you tell the story of a particular movie you loved and that had a massive impact on you. You focus on the story itself, then on your feelings and responses adding particular similarities to your life, if any, and finally how the story has changed you.

The Notebook movie keeps coming to my mind as I write, so let me use this example. You share *The Notebook* story, the emotions around it, the lessons it taught you. You add your own "Notebook" story of your life. This way your audience will be moved even more and guess what? Next time they see the movie or hear about it, there is a big likelihood that they will think of you.

A way to start this prompt could be: "Have you ever been deeply moved by a movie/book?"

Are you ready to MOVE and be MOVED?

Let's experiment with this.

Also, an extra tip here. When you choose the second option, you can choose stories, movies or a book related to your "niche". So, *The Notebook* story could be used if you are a relationship coach for instance.

Storyteller, Teacher

"Social media is a dialogue, not a monologue. Ask questions, reply, engage"

Debora Luzi

Prompt 33: Old and wise

I am so passionate about storytelling. Storytelling is the new HOT trend now on social media and is starting to influence the corporate world too.

Not a surprise since humans have been big storytellers since the beginning of time.

Today I would love to explore some storytelling.

I want you to think about an old wise person in your childhood or early life that has influenced you or given you valuable insights and lessons about life. It could be one of your grandparents, or old neighbours, or someone you just met on a long trip.

Tell us about the encounter, the experience, the details.

Make sure you describe them really well, maybe they had a special smell, or they would walk in a special way, or smile in a certain way.

When you describe them, do it so well that the reader can almost SEE and experience them too.

Then go into exploring your interactions, the talks, the lessons, the learnings.

Then wrap everything beautifully and talk about how those learnings have changed you or transformed you.

A way to start the prompt could be: "He has given me the biggest lesson of my life..."

Just a tip here. As you keep writing, do not give away the lessons in the first few lines. After that entrance, describe the situation, the person, set the scene and then you can develop the lessons, the learnings and close with a final message for your readers.

Storyteller, Teacher

Prompt 34: My name is motivation

The sun feels like hot fire today in London.

So I am all inspired to get things on fire today, especially your motivation towards your audience, prospects and clients.

There is nothing better than a great coach, service provider, practitioner, artist who knows how to motivate and inspire their audience.

Shall we practise some of this motivational muscle?

◈ Close your eyes

◈ Go back to a particular time in your life when you motivated someone to do something

◈ It could be cheering your children at the school sports day or a friend who had just split with her partner

◈ Picture that moment

◈ Step into that beautiful motivating energy you had

Now think about how you can motivate your audience to do something, to take that action they have never taken.

Think about the particular result you deliver and think of how you can motivate your audience to do it.

Maybe it's doing a live video for the first time

Maybe it's saying" no" to someone

Maybe it's setting boundaries for the first time

Maybe it's going to the gym for the first time

How can you motivate them with all your heart and passion?

And when I say motivate I mean the real thing, not just "come on, do it".

Set your words on fire. Show your fire.

✎ Be direct

✎ Be bold

✎ Be real

✎ Be eye-opening

✎ Be firm

✎ Ready?

Let's give this a go.

If it helps, think that you are about to motivate someone whose life is at the last straw. Your words are the only way out they have.

A way to start the prompt could be: "How long are you planning to...(play small, be single or struggle to get clients etc)."

Teacher, Leader

Writing Mantra for today...

My content always stands out

Prompt 35: I promise...

I promise...

Human beings like promises. We look for promises. We give promises. Promises reassure us.

However, as an entrepreneur, we often feel scared to give promises for our work and the results we can deliver. How do I know this? I had fears of making promises myself and I now help my clients to go through the scary "promise" phase.

You see, there is no guarantee out there in the world. I personally was in group programs where some people got results and some didn't. How often do we buy a face cream that guarantees certain results, but we do not get them, while our friend Mary does?

Promises are important in your marketing and messaging. Your audience will want to feel reassured that there is a high chance of them getting the results and promises you claim your offer will bring to them. They will HOPE to get them, and hope is a big influencer when it comes to buying!

Now... it is very important that you have delivered your promises once before, to other clients or to yourself. If you have done it once you can do it twice and also it will help you with getting testimonials to back the promise up.

Many entrepreneurs out there are shy and doubtful about their promise and so their content looks fluffy and a bit all over the place.

Making a promise that you can deliver a certain result is something you totally need to own in your business and stop feeling shy about.

Let's look at how you can develop a promise. I want you to consider some of these questions:

🖉 Have you helped someone to get from A to B?

🖉 Have you helped someone to make a certain amount of money in their business?

🖉 Have you helped someone to find real love and get married?

🖉 Have you helped someone to drop to their ideal weight?

🖉 Have you helped someone to become super confident, do live videos, propose to clients all the time or leave their abusive marriage for instance?

Have a think... Let's explore this and start writing down a few promises you can confidently claim in your business.

Again, be very specific, saying, for instance, "I will help you to be more confident" or "get to your ideal weight" is not enough.

Peel off the layers and you may want to go back and ask your clients about the amazing transformations you brought into their lives.

Gather evidence, private messages from your clients, and testimonials to help you with this and however odd it may seem, do not use the word promise in your marketing.

You can start the prompt with these words: "I am passionate about helping you/guiding you/teaching you to..."

Salesperson

Prompt 36: Possibilities

Let's explore possibilities today.

Two of the main reasons why you or your client do not invest is mainly due to these factors: TIME and MONEY.

These are the biggest objections when it comes to selling your products and services. Often to unblock those limitations all it takes is letting your prospect see the possibilities of what could happen if they had all the time and money in the world.

So, let's dig deep into this today.

Start writing for yourself and as if you were your soul client.

   ✎ What would I do if I had all the time in the world?

   ✎ What would I do if I had all the money in the world?

Let the pen write and do not stop. Give yourself at least 5 minutes of possibilities. Think of all the things you could and would do.

You could use this piece of writing just as practice or you could ask your audience or inner circle this question to see what they would do.

If you do the above, you could use some of their language when you create sales pages, sales content etc.

A few ways to start the prompt could be: "This is what I would do if I had all the time in the world..."or "What would you do if you had all the money (or time) in the world?"

Discoverer, Salesperson

Prompt 37: What do you think?

I used a very powerful writing idea today on my wall.

I asked people to let me know their favourite inspirational song for me to play at the Women Who Dare to Desire Conference.

I did this for a few reasons:

- I really need some song ideas as I am starting the playlist

- I wanted to raise awareness and remind my audience of the conference

- I wanted to boost engagement as I will post a few important posts in the next few days

Now. Let's have a look at this. Many people use this "Technique" of asking their audience questions, but often I see people asking the wrong questions.

When you ask questions you always need to make sure you are in the driving seat and you simply ask for an opinion or advice. You would not ask your audience advice on questions you should know about, related to your business or what you do.

Imagine for instance a style coach asking, "What is the best hat to go with that dress...." Well! She/he should know that!

Asking questions of your audience is very important as it makes them feel part of your journey.

It boosts engagement because people love contributing and replying to questions.

It creates conversations on your wall which is REALLY good for visibility.

I see a lot of people asking something like: "I just did a photoshoot, which pictures shall I add on my website?" or "which logo is best?"

This is so common that I am actually bored with them.

So let's look outside the box and create some questions asking your audience about a simple decision you need to make, or a venue you are trying to find for your event, or their favourite song for your playlist or... or...

Let's get creative.

Is there anything you are creating right now which requires some small piece of advice from your audience?

If you are not a style coach, of course, you can ask which dress is better to wear for your award ceremony.

Discoverer

Prompt 38: Let's splash some cash

Be open about this prompt even if you think it does not resonate with you.

Today I am in a CASH mood.

I just wrote a post on my personal profile with some cash thoughts.

Let's admit it, this word makes many of you feel uncomfortable, and often you avoid talking about cash/money in your RESULTS.

I am guilty of this too.

However, today let's do this exercise.

- ✎ I want you to think first about the SPECIFIC results you bring to your clients

- ✎ Then think of the same results in terms of financial gain or loss

Let me explain.

For instance, even if you are a relationship coach and you bring love to people's life, think about how this will translate into financial gain?

For instance, married couples or couples in relationships save more, buy more assets together, go out less and save more on binge drinking! For instance.

I am brainstorming here. Stay in an open state of mind.

So, what financial impact can your results bring into your clients' life?

We are just exploring here; you may realise that this will open a brand new perspective for you.

For instance, one very successful piece of content I wrote about joining my writing academy was related to the financial gain of joining. I talked about how much money you can save in business coaching and programs by joining the academy as you get business support in there too.

Another example is the wide success of my FREE writing challenge which I run three times a year, "From content to cash", If I had given it the title "from content to success", for instance, it would have less impact and definitely fewer people joining.

This might be a harsh truth for some, but you know what? There is nothing wrong with it.

For now, let's look at the financial benefits of the results you deliver.

Once you have identified them you could start the prompt with:

"Are you ready to save £xxx amount this year?

"This is what you could save by joining my program"

"Are you ready to make some (X amount of) money that will help you to...."

Salesperson

Writing Mantra for today...

I can create content on steroids

Prompt 39: Thank you

You've heard and overheard about gratitude so many times, and today Debora is talking about it too!

You know there could never be enough gratitude in your life, the more you are grateful for, the more of what you are grateful for will show up in your life, the happier you will feel because you will start seeing ONLY the good things that happen to you.

Let's use gratitude as storyteller content today. I want you to start writing with these words...

"Thank you........(and you add the name of a PERSON you are truly grateful for in your life)".

It could be your mum, your dad, a teacher, coach or role model. Get thinking.

Write as if you are:

🖊 writing to them

🖊 talking to them

🖊 recalling the words and the sentences exchanged

🖊 recalling the lessons

🖊 recalling the learnings

Let's see where this will take you.

If you are using this as a piece of content you can ask your audience this question at the end:

"Who are you grateful for in your life today? Tell us the story."

By adding this question, you will make the content not only about you but about your audience too.

Discoverer, Storyteller

"Speak and write as you eat. Aka — show up as you are. If you are messy and eat with your fingers, do not pretend to eat like royals."

Debora Luzi

Prompt 40: Why you? Not again?

Today let's write a story, not any story... but a particular story that your audience must know about you.

It is the story of WHY you do what you do.

I do not know you, but when I listen to speakers or read stories of successful entrepreneurs, I always have a question in mind.

"But how did they get there? What was the catalyst situation or circumstance that made them do what they do?"

And if I am not told this information I feel, somehow, that I cannot connect at a deeper level to this person.

Knowing where it all began for you and your business is vital for your audience and often your "Why I started" story will be similar to your audience and will be a validation to them that yes, you have got courage, you are brave and that you are the person they need.

I want you to go back in time, close your eyes and go back to that very precise moment when you took the decision to start your business.

◈ What was going on in your life at the time?

◈ What was your mind chatter saying?

◈ What were you doing?

◈ Did something bad happen?

◈ What was the straw that broke the camel's back?

Ask yourself these questions and make sure to be specific and descriptive with the situation and your feelings.

Start writing!

And then go and share it with your audience.

Tell them where your business came from.

I am sure they are dying to know, and this will bring them one step closer to you.

A way to start the prompt could be: "You may wonder why I do what I do."

Discoverer, Storyteller, Leader

Writing Mantra for today...

I love to change lives
through my content

Prompt 41: Bomb zone

Are you ready to throw bombs today?

Yes! Let me explain.

As you know you must show your audience that you take a stand, that you are strong (and have flaws too of course) and that you have firm beliefs and ideas. Which is the role of the leader in the 5 writing personalities.

Today I want you think about some ideas and concepts, some truths you believe in around your business and industry. Maybe you see everyone doing X, and it drives you crazy because you know the solution is Y.

The thing is that I am not asking you to write a full piece of content but short sentences which I call truth bombs.

I am sure some of you might feel shy to throw them. If that is the case, I want you to realise that they can help you set your authority and define your expertise.

A few examples could be:

"You believe a funnel, a great sales coach and strategies are the solution to getting more clients in business? Well, think again. You can have it all in place and still have no results because you are missing the right mindset!"

Or

"Affirmations and journaling alone, will not get you where you want to be. It is time you stood up and put those affirmations into action."

Start brainstorming a few, add your vibe, your tone and then be ready to own them and throw them.

A way to start could be: "You believe that......"

Leader

Prompt 42: Shhhh! I have a secret to tell!

Let me tell you a secret. Come closer.

A bit closer please. This is really a big secret.

When I was around 10 years old, I stole a lollipop from a shop with some friends. As we were running out, I felt so guilty that I walked all the way back to the shop and put it back!

Today it's secret time, wonderful writers.

I want you to think about something that people might not know about you, something you may feel a bit ashamed to say. Something that could surprise your audience and inspire them at the same time.

You see, one of the things I always say is that as business owners we are also big entertainers.

Your audience like to know things about you. Things that you will not necessarily speak about. Things that are a bit of a secret. It helps them to connect with you at a deeper level.

I want you to think of a little secret you are hiding. Shhhh! Think of something that has a happy ending and a positive message in the end or a positive lesson you learnt from it.

A few ways to start the prompt are:

"You would never guess this about me..."

"Let me tell you a secret..."

"Can you believe I did this?"

Discoverer, Storyteller, Leader

Prompt 43: The lie and the truth

I came across this beautiful story today and I thought it will give you some inspiration to write your own story.

You know how important it is to always share your story, insights, experiences with your audience? It builds trust and a deeper connection.

So here goes, the story that comes from a 19th Century legend:

" According to a 19th century legend, the Truth and the Lie meet one day. The Lie says to the Truth: "It's a marvellous day today"! The Truth looks up to the skies and sighs, for the day was really beautiful. They spend a lot of time together, ultimately arriving beside a well. The Lie tells the Truth: "The water is very nice, let's take a bath together!" The Truth, once again suspicious, tests the water and discovers that it indeed is very nice. They undress and start bathing. Suddenly, the Lie comes out of the water, puts on the clothes of the Truth and runs away. The furious Truth comes out of the well and runs everywhere to find the Lie and to get her clothes back. The World, seeing the Truth naked, turns its gaze away, with contempt and rage. The poor Truth returns to the well and disappears forever, hiding therein its shame. Since then, the Lie travels around the world, dressed as the Truth, satisfying the needs of society, because, the World, in any case, harbours no wish at all to meet the naked Truth."

I want to ask you..... what lies have you been telling yourself?

What lies are your clients telling themselves?

Write a story either for you or for your client, starting like this:

"I lied to myself every single day..." If you want to write about you

Or

"You realise you have been lying to yourself all along" if you want to write from your soul client point of view.

Remember not to give away all of the story straight after the first sentence.

This could lead to some interesting content.

Discoverer, Storyteller, Salesperson

"Let your audience see the real you. And before you do that, make sure you see you first"

Debora Luzi

Prompt 44: I missed out!

Today I want to explore something rather interesting, the power of missing OUT!

As humans, we naturally hate missing out. I do not know you but when someone tells me they had a great party and I was not there, I feel a bit upset and jealous that I missed it, and I will make sure not to miss it next time.

You can use these powerful tools and experiences in your marketing and message too. I often make my audience "jealous", for not having participated in something I organized, or I show them all the photos of the fun we had.

I do this not only to make them "jealous" and make sure they do not miss out next time but also to show them the journey I take my audience or clients on.

Making your audience aware of what they can potentially miss out on by not joining your group, your event or your products and services can be very beneficial. You can use this principle in sales content, sign up pages or simply by showing your audience the fun and excitement you had with your group, clients etc.

Now, let's go and explore the writing part.

How would you add pieces of "missing out" in your writing?

I advise to not overdo it and always give it your unique flavours. For instance, I quite like to be sarcastic in my writing, so the tone of voice I use might be a bit sarcastic. This does not mean you have to do the same. Adapt the writing to your style.

Let's brainstorm here:

What are your clients MISSING out on NOT working closely with you, or coming to your events etc?

Start writing.

For instance, all the people who did not join the Writing Academy have missed this amazing opportunity of joining for less than £50 per month when the price has now doubled.

They have missed the opportunity to get direct and specific help on their content writing from someone who went from 0 engagement and not being noticed to standing out in the crowd rather quickly.

They have missed the opportunity to save hundreds of pounds on copywriting bills by being their own copywriter.

These are just examples. Now it is your turn.

Think of what your potential clients would miss out on in terms of not working with your expertise.

There is no right or wrong here, my aim is for you to write and see where this piece of writing can take you. You could easily use parts of it and add it to your offers.

A way to start the prompt could be: "You would not want to miss this for the world".

Salesperson

Writing Mantra for today...

Words are the highest
expression of my truth

Prompt 45: Surprise, surprise!

Surprise! Surprise!

Yes, I literally ask you to go back to a time in your life when someone or something really surprised you.

Was it a special birthday surprise? Was it your mum gifting you a puppy when you were little?

Go back to that exact moment and describe it in every little detail.

Be as descriptive as possible. Recall the conversations, the smells, the sights, the words of excitement. Remember the expressions on your and other people's faces.

Now, think about the surprise factor. People love surprises. Your audience will love surprises.

Do you ever surprise your audience with something special they truly want?

Do you ever keep them waiting for something you are going to give to them?

How can you surprise them today? What surprise party are you planning for them?

A way to start the prompt could be: "I am going to surprise you today!"

Discoverer, Salesperson

Prompt 46: I feel

Get a pen and paper. Sit in a quiet place and just write nonstop for at least 8 minutes. Start with these words:

"TODAY I FEEL..."

Simply write whatever comes up. And remember that any feelings are accepted.

However you feel, write about it for at least 8 minutes. If you feel upset it is almost guaranteed that after the 8 minutes you will feel much better, and if you feel happy after the 8 minutes you will feel even happier.

Why are we doing this, what is the purpose of writing about our feelings when we need to focus on our clients instead and his/her feelings?

Remember that sharing how you feel with your audience is important.

Before you tell your audience what you do, tell them who you are.

Get used to sharing your feelings often with your audience. Maybe you have felt frustrated about something, or doubtful about a new project, or vulnerable about stepping up your game?

Make sure to share those feelings, always from the victorious side and not that of the victim.

Make sure that every time you share your feelings, you share them with the intent of inspiring your audience, teaching them a lesson or motivating them.

Do not share your feelings from a place of hate, resentment or revenge.

You may want to get into the habit of writing this prompt at least once a week to check in with yourself and what goes on in your world. You will be surprised at how many realisations, ideas, steps forward this prompt can create for you.

Discoverer.

"Trust who you are. Trust every inch of it and show up with it"

Debora Luzi

Prompt 47: Competitions are back in fashion

Competitions are such an exciting way to give some of your products away, to get new clients, new followers, new email addresses.

I want to invite you to create an exciting competition with one of your products and services as a giveaway.

First of all, start thinking what your intention is for doing a competition (apart from because Debora is asking you to do it as part of this prompt). What do you want to get out of it? More emails, more people trying your services, more people into your funnel, a buzz around your business?

Now think about the WHAT. What are you actually giving away (free session, PDF with 5/10 tips, a space in your next workshop, a free month's membership?)

Give away something you want to create awareness around.

Next think about the timing: this is key to building momentum. How long will this last, when will the winner be announced?

Then focus on documenting the activities of the competition, which means telling stories, facts about the competition, how many people signed up, what is the response you are getting etc.

Now let's go into the writing skills of writing the actual content.

You need a strong headline such as GIVE AWAY, FREE SESSION, or WIN. These may sound boring, but they work as they help you to grab people's attention. Let's admit it. Who does not like a freebie? Go straight to the point and be very specific on what it is that you are giving away.

Mention the benefits of what you are giving away (what will this do for the reader, why do they need this?)

Be original in all of this, how can you spice things up?

Here are some ideas for you.

You can share a short story of why you have decided to run this competition. You could get all the participants to be live with you when you do the draw and announce the winners. Make the participants take an action to enter the competition and publish a picture of them taking the action and ask them to tag you. This is a great way to create awareness around you and your business.

Write a piece of content with a giveaway and share it with your audience.

Be creative and original. Add any crazy ideas that might come to your mind and ask people to share with their friends and family and spread the love.

I am going to create a great competition around the 2nd birthday of The Writing Academy for Entrepreneurs. I am going to give away to a lucky person, a one-month free membership. I will make people enter the competition and to filter out the timewasters I am going to ask people to answer a very simple question. Then I will create a buzz around it and go live announcing the winner and creating suspense throughout the video.

Salesperson

Writing Mantra for today...

I write authentically and
unapologetically

Prompt 48: Interviewing you!

Visualisation is one of the most powerful tools you can use to make things happen in your life.

Imagine you were a journalist and you have just interviewed yourself in 5 years' time.

In the interview, focus on the amazing success you had, all the achievements you have had, the mistakes you made along the way and all the people you are thankful for in the journey.

Remember to write in the third person.

This is an example to give you an idea:

"Today I had the pleasure of interviewing mum of three and daring woman Debora Luzi on her way to success and owning a 7 figure business and impacting millions of women around the world."

One way you could use this prompt is to share with your audience your vision, your ambitions and your goals.

People often feel shy and scared to say out loud what they desire to achieve in case of looking too pretentious or in case it doesn't happen. Let me tell you, showing your audience that you have a big vision and that you are determined to go after it, will only motivate and inspire them to do the same.

You can start the prompt with the words above "Today I had the pleasure of interviewing..." or you could just share your vision... "I have a vision..." and at the end you can ask your audience "What is yours?"

Discoverer, Leader

Prompt 49: Internal dialogue

Have you ever actually written down a full conversation between your inner voices?

I did and I do so many times. There is something so special and eye-opening about doing this.

Let's have a look at some psychology behind it first.

When you actually give a shape or a persona to your inner negative voices, they become less scary to your eyes and mind.

Why? Imagine entering a dark room where you have been told there are lots of monsters, but you do not know what these monsters look like. You start wondering and feeling really scared of the unknown.

Now, imagine you are in a dark room, you know there are monsters in there and suddenly the light is turned on and you can quickly see where the monsters are and what they look like. Then the light goes off again.

This time you will feel safer and less scared because you know more.

The same happens when you start to give life to your inner voices and even write them down in a dialogue. These voices will lose a lot of their power once you define them and bring them to the light.

I use a lot of direct speech in my writing and share real conversations that happen in my mind to engage my audience more and to make the whole content easier to read.

Let's have some fun. Write a full dialogue between your inner voices. You pick which ones. It could be between two bad ones wanting to win the negativity trophy or between a good and a bad one just trying to help you decide on an action you want to take.

It could go like this:

Voice 1 "I told you it would not work, but you did not listen."

Voice 2 "Yes because I am tired of you and you know I am stubborn anyway."

Voice 1 "Well keep being stubborn and failing. If I were you, I would no longer show up."

Voice 2 "Maybe you are right."

Voice 1 "Oh! You decided to listen. Good. That is what I am here for. To keep you safe."

Be creative with the story and make it real. Make your inner voices have a discussion.

A way to start the prompt could be: "Sometimes I do not know who to listen to" or "Today I had a real fight going on in my head over an action I had to take."

Discoverer, Storyteller

"Picasso did not go like "Let me check what Monet is doing". He just started to paint from his own mind"

Debora Luzi

Prompt 50: The number ONE lesson

Today I want you to imagine this:

You are being interviewed by a top magazine editor for a feature in their magazine.

The editor asks you lots and lots of questions and then he/she comes to the last question before closing the interview.

The question is:

"What is the number one lesson that life has given you?"

Such a beautiful question but also rather challenging to answer because I am sure life has given you more than one lesson.

I want you to focus on ONE lesson, one teaching, one concept and write about it.

What would that be?

Maybe you want to focus on a sentence like "If life gives you lemons, make lemonade"[4] or "Life isn't about waiting for the storm to pass; it's about learning how to dance in the rain"[5].

These are just to give you an idea.

---

4. Originally by the American writer Elbert Hubbard (1856-1915) in an obituary he wrote for the actor Marshall Pinckney Wilder. However, it is often attributed to Dale Carnegie who used something similar in his book *How to Stop Worrying and Start Living*

5. Vivien Greene (1904-2003) British writer, widow of the novelist Graham Greene and world authority on dolls' houses..

Here are some guidelines on how to develop the content or go as wild as you like if you already have an idea on what to write.

✐ Ideas to start:
"This is the number one lesson that life has given me so far" or "This is my number one lesson in life, what is yours?" or create your own

✐ Do not give away the idea straight away, go back to the moment when you realised this lesson was important for you. Share a little story linked to you getting this lesson

✐ Say what the lesson is

✐ Deliver the final message about this lesson to your audience. You could ask questions like "what is yours" or "Has life ever given you this lesson?"

Discoverer, Storyteller

Writing Mantra for today...

I own my writing voice fully

Prompt 51: I am different and I know it!

A strong positioning in your business is key.

You create a strong positioning by:

- standing out
- showing that you are different
- showing that you give a lot of value
- showing that you are the expert
- showing that what you teach works
- showing that you stand against what everyone else is doing.

I want you to think about your particular field in your business.

Think about how everyone talks about the same things, offers the same processes and results.

How are you *different* from them?

What is the thing that *everyone* teaches in your field and that you stand against and that you do differently?

Let me give you an example here:

For instance, all intuitive business coaches teach about following our intuition and taking inspired actions and are thought not to focus too much on the plan or the strategy.

Wrong! You need intuition and strategy to make your business work as one or the other will not work alone.

Or the mindset coach who focuses on getting the right mindset first then goes out there and does business. Totally wrong! As your mindset will never be READY and DONE!

Now is your turn.

Think of how your method or process is different from anybody else's and start writing about it.

You can start writing using these words:

"Why is my method different, you may ask?"

Discoverer, Leader

Prompt 52: I am about to BURST with URGENCY

This prompt is absolutely urgent! Do it NOW or if not, it will disappear from this page within 3 minutes of you reading it.

I got you! I am just kidding.

I want you to imagine getting inside the head of your soul clients to find out what their BUY NOW URGENCY button is.

Today I want you to think about the URGENCY of buying what you are selling from the point of view of your soul client.

🖋 What is the urgency of your soul client?

🖋 WHY do they need to buy NOW?

🖋 What happens if THEY DO NOT BUY NOW?

Answer the questions above and really think about the urgent words you can use.

Working on your clients' URGENCY is vital so that you can understand which WORDS will make them buy your products and services and act NOW.

Start the prompt like this:

"You think this is not urgent enough....think again!"

'Why you must act now.....''

Storyteller

"Say it and write it now.
Tomorrow is too late"

Debora Luzi

Prompt 53: Movie time

Awwww! Today, wonderful writers, we are going to have a bit of fun and we will pretend to play the role of.....

The producer!

Yes, exactly. Today YOU are a producer and film director of your own movie and you are going to SET THE SCENES for your wonderful new movie.

And what is the movie about? YOUR SOUL CLIENT!

Yes!

Let's take a step back.

I want you to IMAGINE all the possible scenarios your soul clients are IN daily. I want you to think about all the scenes, circumstances they live daily.

So, we are going into DEEP details here. And I mean deep....

Details are like the clothes she is wearing, the things she/he carries, her home, the mess or not, the setup of the rooms, the supermarket she/he goes to, the places she/he goes to, or doesn't go to.

Today we are worrying ONLY about the SCENES, not dialogue or conversations. You can express the FEELINGS she feels inside.

Why are we doing this? Because you want to set yourself apart from the others and make your soul client KNOW THAT YOU GET HER or HIM down to the small details.

You want to make her or him KNOW that you KNOW exactly WHAT she/he is going through.

We are going to describes the scenes of her/his daily life.

I give you some examples.

🖊 The curtains in the bedroom are drawn, the bedside table lamp is on, but she puts a t-shirt on top of it to dim the light as she cannot bear to see herself in the mirror which is just above the lamp. Clothes are spread all over the floor as she has not left the room for 3 days. A strong smell of damp and old is all over the room (I am inventing here)

🖊 She leaves the house in her baggy clothes for the short walk to the supermarket. The car is parked outside, cobwebs all over the front mirror as she has not used the car in days. She walks looking down and goes to the nearest supermarket, even if it is the most expensive as she cannot bear to walk further

🖊 She silently enters the room. For a moment she wants to leave. The room is full of women smiling and drinking champagne, celebrating. She has nothing to celebrate. For a moment she wants to turn back, but she decides to stay. Her jacket is an old grey jacket, just like the colour of her soul. She takes it off and makes for the toilet

🖊 She is at the restaurant with other friends. Somehow she managed to accept the invitation, even though she did not want to. All her friends are smiling and enjoying themselves. All she worries about is the moment the waiter arrives to take the order. She is not hungry. She suddenly thinks about all the delicious food that is going to tempt her stomach. Full of anxiety she stares at the waiters bringing all those delicious dishes up and down. She has not eaten properly for a few weeks and has managed to shed 1kg. A draught comes from the door; someone is leaving, she wants to run away

These are ideas to help you get closer to your soul client and to start writing this type of scenario on your sales copy. These might be too long for a post but you can review them and get the idea.

Let the pen flow and see what will come out of this. Stay open always.

Storyteller, Salesperson

Prompt 54: Engagement boost

Today we are going to get your audience very engaged, gorgeous writers.

Are you ready?

Let's give your audience some options they can choose from.

There are many ways you can do this.

The classic is to give option A, B, C. So for instance you can ask a question related to what you do and the results you bring and ask your audience to choose from options A, B, C.

It does not have to be a question only related to what you do, it could be a curious question asking about their personality or character for instance.

A funny option would be to ask them to choose a character. An example here. I could ask: Who do you feel like when you go on sales conversations?

Joan of Arc, bring it on!

Scaredy cat, I do it but I shake all the way!

Or Frozen, yes you get utterly frozen!

Another option would be to ask a question and ask them if they feel like a fruit for instance or an animal.

This way you bring fun into your question and people will be willing to play the game.

So let's brainstorm some questions first and then select the different options, either just with a letter or with some twist as explained above (choosing characters, movie stars, fruits, animals etc)

Ready?

Let's get some engagement going.

Discoverer, Teacher

"It is not about silencing another's voice with yours. It is about inspiring others to raise theirs"

Debora Luzi

Prompt 55: I love metaphors

Gorgeous writers, are you ready to explore something today?

We will explore this particular "thing' in detail as I want you to get very familiar with it and start using it in your writing.

What am I talking about?

Metaphors!

Yes metaphors are all around us, they are everywhere and we see, feel, smell, hear and touch them all the time.

Metaphors help us to understand more easily the world around us and its meaning.

Many of your memories and subconscious memories are linked to metaphors. People learn new things by associating them with existing ideas, visions, and experiences.

Metaphors allow your readers to "understand better" and to relate to whatever you want to explain or tell better.

Just in case you wonder.....

Look at these two sentences:

"I feel amazing"

or

"I feel on top of the world"

Which one sounds more powerful and which one will you probably connect to deeper?

The second one, right? Why? Because by saying that, you are engaging the vision, you are "seeing" you or someone else on top of a mountain for instance or a cloud or the world itself.

So let's play!

I want to invite you to explore metaphors related to the results you bring your clients.

Some help here on how to do this:

First, write down the results you bring

Then research on the internet a few metaphors and make some up yourself. Mix and match them.

See which one you can use to match the results you bring...

So for instance:

- You will no longer feel like a fish out of water in the online world after joining my program. You will feel like the world is your stage when it comes to showing up online.

- It is time you take the reins of your life back in your hand, and become the lead role.

- You are to crown yourself with power and self-beliefs and become the queen of your queendom.

I am just inventing here.

Imagine how much you can play with this.

Just a few top tips here:

Metaphors linked to the five senses are very powerful, especially the ones related to taste and touch!

Ready? Let's see where your imagination takes you!

I am so excited about this.

You do not need to write a whole post or a long content, just a few ideas are fine which you can insert into your content material.

Discoverer, Storyteller, Teacher, Leader and Salesperson

Prompt 55 and 1: Let's make some sums

Wow, you have made it to the end!

In this last prompt I would love you to grab pen and paper and share your experience of this book.

I do not know you, but I am a big fan of reading real books that I can scribble on and highlight the most important concepts with different colours.

If the book I am reading is very practical and full of information I even rewrite the most important parts in a separate notebook dedicated just for the book, so that I can go back to it without having to read the book again.

How many times have you read a book, enjoyed it, felt so fired up to take action and make changes only to forget all about it after a few days?

I certainly have.

It is my intention to not make that happen with this book.

I hope you will keep coming back to it and put all the many teachings and ideas into practice.

To help you do that I had this idea of ending the last prompt with a beautiful summary.

I would love you to think about all the new things, ideas and perceptions you have encountered throughout this book and start thinking how these ideas have and will change the way you write from now on.

As I say "Do not overthink it, let the pen flow".

You can start the prompt with these words:

"As a consequence of reading this book from now on I WILL..."

✐ What changes will you make?

✐ What new ideas will you be implementing?

✐ How brave will you become when it comes to writing content?

✐ Who is the new "YOU" you will be writing about?

I suggest you write this prompt on a separate piece of paper you can keep going back to. You may want to stick this prompt to your office wall or somewhere visible which you can see every day.

This is your promise to yourself. This is the metamorphosis that will happen to the writer in you.

This is the beginning of a new writing experience.

This is the release of your deepest, most beautiful writing voice.

May you start to trust it and love it, because when you do, your audience will too.

THE JOURNEY HAS ONLY JUST BEGUN

I sincerely hope you have enjoyed writing all the prompts, dear writer. As you can see, writing ideas can be born out of anything. It is my biggest wish for you to keep writing and to not stop here. You may feel lost now that you have no more prompts and ideas to use. If you do, I just want to remind you how easy it is to just grab pen and paper and write. When you remove the should, the prejudices, the fears, the pen has no other means than that of flowing freely onto the paper.

I will probably write book number 2 and give you many more prompts and ideas but until then I encourage you to use your imagination. Remember my number one rule is this: you can create content out of anything.

And I would love to hear from you. Let me know what your favourite prompt was and why and which one gave you the most engagement.

I would love to know all the internal realisations you might have had along the way, the "aha" moments, the engagement you received from your writing and the impact that you have made on your audience with this new way of writing.

Feel free to tag my name through my Facebook Business page name "Debora Luzi" in your social media content when you share the prompts with your audience.

And could I kindly ask you to like my page? That would be daramazing.

Ultimately, I would love you to share the love for this book and all the learnings with others. The world needs more freedom of expression and less fear in speaking one's truth.

May you have found that freedom of expression and that excitement for writing.

With much daring and written love,

Debora Luzi

ABOUT THE AUTHOR

Debora is the daring inner voice mentor, passionate about teaching and guiding entrepreneurs to speak and write their truest, most authentic voice so that their clients can find and choose them.

She is the founder of the Women Who Dare to Desire Conference, a centre stage for visionary women who are ready to inspire the world by sharing their stories and messages.

Debora founded The Writing Academy for Entrepreneurs in May 2018 following an intuitive whisper while looking for a place where entrepreneurs could share their writing, learn more about how to write content that connects, converts and impacts, and find their unique writing voice. As she could not find such a place, she created one.

The Writing Academy has members from all over the world.

Debora is also a passionate speaker who organises regular speaking events called "Dare the Stage" where people can improve their speaking skills through improvisations, role-play, games and acting.

Debora is a mother to three boys, a passionate salsa dancer, and lives in London with her children and husband.

ABOUT THE WRITING ACADEMY FOR ENTREPRENEURS

The Writing Academy for Entrepreneurs is the only online community focused exclusively on content creation for entrepreneurs.

Debora teaches and inspires entrepreneurs from any writing background and with any writing skills to write their very own unique, raw and authentic content which converts and impacts.

The Writing Academy is a magical place of learning and growth for any entrepreneur who would like to show up more, discover their creativity and write in the most natural way possible.

Debora delivers two writing prompts a week. Each prompt is not only a writing idea but a value in itself. Debora shares her knowledge of how certain content works better than others, how to use persuasion and what type of content to use depending on each specific business goal.

There are over 20 recorded pieces of training in the academy library including how to pitch an idea to the press, how to get more engagement in your content, how to create a Facebook ad that converts, how to create weekly and monthly content and many more.

Two more training sessions are delivered in the academy each month. One by Debora and another by special guest speakers.

Through the feature, #sharemywords, members can share their writing for feedback and analysis.

There is an 'accountability partner' system in place where each member is paired with someone else in the academy.

Also, there is a strong focus on writing articles for your own blog, online publications and magazines of your choice.

Debora opens the door to the Writing Academy three times a year through a wonderful and inspiring FREE 5 days writing challenge called "From Content to Cash".

Make sure to follow Debora on social media for updates on the challenge launch.

To join or find out more about it, check here: www.deboraluzi.com/writing-academy.

TESTIMONIALS FOR DEBORA'S WORK

I have been in Debora's writing academy for over a year. I first discovered the power of writing on her challenge. I found it very healing. The amount of engagement I had compared for my usual posts was incredible. It completely cured any fear i had of getting visible. In fact, if I had it my way I would create content all day. I love the prompts Debora gives us on a weekly basis. I always learn from her from her coaching and prompts but also watch her as living proof of what she teaches. I find Debora really inspires me. She attracts really great people too. I really love the group Q&A calls we do with people like me. I would not hesitate to recommend the academy. It is worth its's weight in gold!

Deborah Mendes
Nature Inspired Business Mentor

I have been a proud member of Debora Luzi Writing Academy for Entrepreneurs, for the last 2 years, being part of the academy has developed my content skills and visibility for my business in all social medias' platforms. The trainings in the academy and live writing sessions really support my own personal growth in ways I could have not anticipated. Being part of the Academy has made me more confident, more daring and definitely has propelled me to follow my desires. Working with Debora Luzi you are guaranteed that you will be taking consistent actions in your business and you will experience exponential growth.

Lucia Margarida Pestana
Career Coach and HR Professional

I took part in Debora's 'Create It, Nail It, Sell It' workshop this week. I love the way Debora created space for everyone to explore and evolve their core message - and then take this forward into planning and promotional activities aimed at business growth.

She has a real talent for listening and suggesting improvements to words - or a single word - that focus emotional engagement.

Highly recommended. Thank you.

Lynne Stainthorpe
Brand Strategist at Big Idea Brand Marketing

Debora teaches about writing copies that work. She gives us tools that bring attention. She is a copy genius. I am evolving in my writing. Debora is really amazing at what she does.

Agnieszka Burban
Relationship Expert

CONTACT DEBORA

You can contact Debora in the following ways:

www.deboraluzi.com

www.deboraluzi.com/writing-academy

info@deboraluzi.com

www.facebook.com/deboraluzicoachingandhealing

www.linkedin.com/in/debora-luzi-79081b29/

www.instagram.com/deboraluziofficial/

ACKNOWLEDGEMENTS

I would like to share a massive thank you to all the members of my writing academy, who are trusting me every day to help them unleash their writing genius.

A particular thanks to many of them who joined me from the very beginning when I had not figured out yet, what I was doing.

Thanks to my audience, and all the people who like my content daily. Thank you so much for reading and stopping by, you make my writing so worthwhile.

A big thanks to the Branding Queen, Desislava Dobreva, who planted the seed idea for this book, helped me believe in my writing and my academy, and for all her content teachings.

Thank you to my husband, Orlando, for putting up with all the moments the whisper talked to me and I had to grab a pen and paper and write, no matter the circumstances. And for reminding me in many down moments that when you do what you love with great passion everything will simply fall into place.

Thanks to my beautiful children, Jazz, Kian and Romeo who are my daily inspirations, my strength, the reason why I do what I do.

Thanks to Lidia, one of the kindest persons I ever met. Thanks for always treating me like your own daughter, for being there for me on those dark moments when I became a single mother and I had no family around. You supported me in following my dreams by helping me to go to all those courses, training and events. I would not be where I am today if it wasn't for you and all your love and support.

Thanks to my dear friend Tina for her love and support and for all those endless WhatsApp messages which kept me sane while building my business and writing this book.

Thanks to my dear friend Samantha for her support and for always being such a strong inspiration.

Thanks to my publisher Sarah Houldcroft for helping me make my vision for this book real. I knew from the first moment I met you we were going to do business together.

Thanks to you dear reader who has picked up this book and trusted me to take you into this beautiful writing journey. I hope to meet you face to face one day and to grab a pen and write with you soon.

Printed in Great Britain
by Amazon

71761049R00183